More Than Poutine

Favourite Foods from My Home and Native Land

Marie Porter

Photography by
Michael Porter

Celebration Generation

www.celebrationgeneration.com

More Than Poutine

First Edition, October 2017

I.S.B.N. 978-0-9976608-4-5

Published and Distributed by

Celebration Generation, LLC
P.O. Box 22315
Robbinsdale, MN 55422

www.celebrationgeneration.com

Cover Photos, Clockwise from Top left:

Rotisserie Chicken Sauce, page 134
Bloody Caesar , page 171
Nanaimo Bars , page 180
Peameal Bacon, page 21
Candy Bars, from page 58

Back Cover Photo:

Tiger Tail Ice Cream, page 220

Acknowledgments

Usually, I start off my acknowledgments with a shout out to my husband, but this time around, the first person I need to thank... isn't actually a person.

This book wouldn't be possible without Canada. While not a person, growing up in Canada shaped me, made me who I am - both as a person, and in the kitchen. Living in one of the most ethnically diverse countries in the world gave me an appreciation for so many cuisines, and I have had almost unlimited opportunity to engage with - and learn from - such a beautiful variety of people, from every imaginable background.

With everything going on in the world today, I have never been more proud to be a Canadian. Happy 150th, Canada! This book is a birthday gift - and love letter - to you.

***

As always, my husband was absolutely instrumental in the development of this book, in many ways - photographer, guinea pig, dish washer, and as emotional support. In this case, he was also "driver": going along on several road trips back home, to acquire source material. He even gave in to my ridiculous assertion that we needed to make one last trip, specifically to buy a doughnut. I married well.

***

Though she is no longer around to see this book completed, my grandmother had a part in its creation... way back in the day. From cooking with me, to bugging her neighbour for traditional Ukranian recipes, to teaching me how to make perogies...

Thank you for everything. Rest in peace.

***

As this book was the result of a very successful Kickstarter campaign, I have 469 backers to thank, en masse. It would not have happened without their help, for not only financial support, but also promotional help and feedback on development.

So, big thanks go to those who supported the campaign for More Than Poutine. Without that initial support, we wouldn't be here again, with a new book!

***

Finally, thank you to all of the Canadians - both at home and away - that contributed requests and feedback for this book. In particular, big thanks to my friend Karine Charlebois for her contribution of 2 recipes - a first for one of my cookbooks!

Table of Contents

Foreword

Mike Myers has been quoted as saying "There is no one more Canadian than a Canadian who no longer lives in Canada".

In my experience - 11 years of living away - that quote is not only true in the general sense, it's especially true when is comes to Canadian foods. Canadian expats may be divided by politics, geography, or even regional culture ... But post a photo of a hideous "poutine" you found in an American restaurant to a Canadian Expat group, and you will find 100% agreement that it's an abomination.

Post about butter tarts, or peameal bacon, and you're guaranteed a long, wistful discussion about the many foods we miss from the motherland. Sure, some people may be anti-raisin weirdos (I tease!) when it comes to butter tarts, but - in general - Canadian food is the great equalizer, a very popular topic of discussion, and a bonding experience.

The thing is, perception of what exactly "Canadian Food" is varies widely, depending on who's being asked.

Having lived in the United States for more than ten years, I'm very aware of the fact that the non-Canadian knowledge of Canadian food tends to begin and end with "poutine". As any Canadian who's lived in the US can attest ... those quotation marks are necessary!

Ask a Canadian who has always lived in Canada about Canadian food, and they will likely also bring up poutine... as well as butter tarts, Nanaimo bars, and - depending on their region - possibly tourtière.

When you ask a Canadian who is a current or former expat, though... be prepared for much more varied responses. As I mentioned earlier, we do miss our butter tarts... but you're far more likely to also hear about regional delicacies, and mass-produced convenience foods. "You don't know what you've got til it's gone" applies both in the appreciation sense, and in the knowledge sense - a lot of the time, we don't tend to realize what is Canadian-specific, until we move away.

Having been spoiled by access to amazing game meats while living in Newfoundland, I'm not at all surprised at how many Canadian expats miss moose stew, caribou bourguignon, flipper pie, and more. You could buy premade rabbit pie in grocery stores there - something I've certainly never seen in Minneapolis!

Flipper pie wouldn't even be legal in the US, due to import restrictions on anything to do with seals. I miss partridgeberries and bakeapples, though I have managed to come up with a partridgeberry substitute (Faux Partridgeberry Wine recipe, page 166).

Expats from other areas lament the lack of access to other natural delicacies. Nova Scotians in particular tend to miss their wild blueberries, the flavour of which is undoubtedly affected by the area's terroir. Fiddle heads, goose berries, blackcurrants, particular types of freshwater fish - there's no end to nature's bounty back home.

Then, there's the matter of missing Canadian foods that don't originate in Canada at all!

One huge influence on Canadian food is Canadian culture in general. Canada's culture is seen as a "cultural mosaic", rather than a melting pot. While this may seem like a minor difference - maybe even semantics - to those who haven't lived elsewhere, it actually has a huge impact on life, the intermingling of various cultures, and - yes - food.

Proper perogies, cabbage rolls, souvlaki, and roti are high on the list of missed "Canadian" foods for many expats, but are Ukrainian, Greek, and Indian in origin. Jamaican beef patties were a common lunch food for me in high school, and almost impossible for me to find in Minneapolis for most of my stay there - later on, I was able to find them at a dollar store, but that's about it.

When your cultural fabric is made up of unique cultures that retain their identity, rather than being expected to "melt in" and assimilate, their foods end up becoming part of the Canadian identity as well. So, while Souvlaki isn't actually Canadian, it's in this book to satisfy the requests of many Canadian expats who are unable to find decent souvlaki in their areas. Same goes for perogies, as the perogies I've found in Minneapolis have all been... sad. As a Winnipegger, I am firmly of the belief that no one should be stuck with sad perogies!

All around, my experiences as an expat Canadian have really given me a chance to think about - and really appreciate - Canadian food.

As my final cookbook project before moving home - and as my own personal way of celebrating Canada's 150th birthday - I wanted to write a book for us.

For those of us who not only crave our tourtière and buttertarts, but would give anything to do shots of Chalet Sauce again.

For those of us who die a little inside when we see what is sold as "Canadian Bacon" - anemic little rounds of ham, not the robust deliciousness of the back bacon we once knew.

For those of us who have caved to craving and paid $3-4+ for a Wunderbar, shipped from Amazon.

For those of us who have given up on ordering "poutine" abroad, knowing full well that there's a chance that whatever ends up being presented may not even involve cheese curds, and will likely end up with a fried egg - or some other nonsense - on top.

One of my favourite "Autistic Superpowers" has always been my ability to taste something, and know what's in it, be able to discern ingredient proportions, and be able to replicate it. It's served me well, living away from home... and I'm so proud to be able to put it to use on a grander scale!

Whether you are an expat looking for a taste of home, a Canadian-in-Canada looking to learn more about regional specialties - or how to make your favourites gluten-free - or a non-Canadian looking to learn more about Canadian food, I hope you enjoy this book!

- Marie Porter

A Note on Balance:

You may notice that this book is a bit unbalanced in terms of types of recipes covered - leaning heavily towards the junk food/dessert end of the spectrum. Well, just as Canadian food is shaped by the land and its kaleidoscope of people, the expat view of Canadian food is similarly affected by their change in life experience. Moving away from home is a lot of stress, even in the best of circumstances. Given the current political climate, I am not in the least bit surprised at the expat focus on comfort foods!

A Note on Recipe Titles:

A good number of recipes in this book are accurate replicas of commercially available, mass produced goods ... so, trademarks come into play.

As such, I've had to get a bit creative with naming this recipes. Have fun connecting the dots, and figuring out where I took inspiration from!

A Note on Gluten:

The vast majority of recipes in this book are either inherently gluten-free, or are gluten free with a simple change of ingredient (eg: use gluten-free beer, use gluten-free soy sauce). Of the remaining recipes, most can be made gluten free, with a certain mixture of flours, which are stated at the end of the recipe. If a recipe makes no mention of gluten, it is inherently gluten free.

Bannock

Breakfast & Brunch

Bannock

Bannock is one of the very first things they taught us to make in school, as we learned about First Nations history. It's a yeast free bread - almost a biscuit - that is simple and easy to make just about anywhere.

While I learned to make it in an oven, historically it was made over an open fire - either in a pan or wrapped around a stick. You can make this at home in a cast iron pan, on a baking sheet (I prefer baking sheet), or while camping. It's great as a breakfast food with a bit of jam, as an accompaniment for French Canadian Pea Soup (page 93), or with game meats.

I use lard, as that's how I was taught - butter can be very expensive in Canada, and isn't "traditional" in the strictest sense... but then again, neither is refined flour.

Makes about 8 servings

All purpose flour	3 cups	750 ml
Baking powder	4 tsp	20 ml
Salt	1 tsp	5 ml
Lard or shortening	1/3 cup	75 ml
Cold water	~1 cup	~ 250 ml

Preheat oven to 400 F (200 C), line a baking sheet with parchment paper.

In a large bowl, mix together dry ingredients. Use two forks or your (clean!) hands to cut the lard into the dry mixture. You'll want it evenly distributed, small bits. Add water to the mix, just enough to bring it together into a dough. Knead lightly to smooth it out a little - don't overwork it, or it will turn out dense.

On the lined baking sheet, gently form dough into a relatively even round, about 1" thick. Bake for about 20 minutes, or until golden brown. Serve warm, with butter... drizzled with honey or maple syrup, or slathered in a nice jam.

For Gluten-free: Mix together 1 ½ cup Light buckwheat flour, ½ cup sorghum flour, 1/3 cup Potato starch, 1/3 cup sweet rice flour, 2 Tbsp tapioca starch. Use in place of all-purpose flour. Increase water slightly. Allow to sit for 10 minutes, covered, before forming onto baking sheet.

Ployes

While these work up like pancakes or crepes - and look sort of like a pancake or crepe - they're actually used as a flatbread in New Brunswick.

When served alongside Fricot (Page 95), it's almost like an Acadian version of injera. When spread with fillings - butter, maple syrup, jam, molasses, cretons (Page 24), etc - and rolled up, it's sort of a New Brunswick analog to the Norwegian Lefse. It makes a fun breakfast food.

In the region, yellow buckwheat flour - made from silverskin buckwheat - is used. It can be difficult to find, outside of the area... so I use light buckwheat flour.

Hint: Ployes rhymes with "toys". The singular is "ploye" and rhymes with "toy".

Makes about 10-12 8" ployes

Light buckwheat flour	2 cups	500 ml
All purpose flour	1 cup	250 ml
Baking powder	1 Tbsp	15 ml
Salt	1 tsp	5 ml
Cold water	1 ½ cups	375 ml
Boiling water	2 cups	500 ml

In a medium or large mixing bowl, combine dry ingredients. Add cold water, whisk until well combined. Allow to rest for 10 minutes.

After 10 minutes is up, add boiling water - slowly and carefully - whisking until well combined, smooth, and runny.

Heat griddle to medium, turn down to medium-low. You don't want the ployes to brown too much before they actually cook. Pour 1/3 cup amounts of batter onto a hot griddle, swirling out to make an 8" round. Allow to cook until top is bubbly and looks dry, about 3 minutes. Do not flip!

Remove from heat, cover with a tea towel, and repeat to use up the rest of the batter. Be sure to stir the batter right before making each subsequent ploye.

Serve hot.

For Gluten-free: Omit all purpose flour. Increase light buckwheat flour to 2 1/3 cups, add 1/3 cup sorghum flour, and 1/4 cup sweet rice flour.

Ployes

Montreal Style Bagels

Montreal Style Bagels

Montreal bagels are more rustic looking, sweeter, and chewier than their non-Montreal counterparts. Visually, they are less plump, have a larger hole in the middle, and tend to be topped in either poppy seeds or sesame seeds - not with an endless variety of toppings.

They are served hot and generally eaten more like a soft pretzel, than how most eat bagels. They're eaten as-is or torn apart, rather than being sliced open

The sweetness comes both from the malt extract powder* in the dough, and from being boiled in a honeyed water solution. Technically, they have to be baked in a wood fire oven in order to be considered legit, but for the purposes of satisfying cravings... well, I won't tell anyone if you don't!

Makes 12-15

Warm - not hot - water	1 ½ cups	375 ml
Active dry yeast	4 tsp	20 ml
Sugar	1/3 cup	75 ml
All purpose flour	4 ½ cups	1125 ml
Malt extract powder	1 Tbsp	15 ml
Large eggs	2	2
Large egg yolk	1	1
Vegetable oil	1/4 cup	50 ml
Water	1 gallon	4 L
Liquid honey	1/3 cup	75 ml
Poppy seeds and/or sesame seeds		

Stir yeast and sugar into warm water, allow to stand for 10 minutes – it should get very bubbly.

In a large mixing bowl, combine flour and malt powder. Pour in yeast mixture, 1 egg, yolk, and vegetable oil, stir well to combine.

Dump dough out onto a floured surface, knead until soft and elastic, 5-10 minutes. Once dough is fully kneaded, place dough in a greased bowl, cover with plastic wrap, and allow to rise for one hour, or until doubled in size.

Once dough has doubled, punch it down, and divide it out into 12-15 equal sized balls. 12 will get you larger bagels that can be sliced/used as normal bagels, 15 gets more authentically sized bagels.

Preheat oven to 425 F (220 C)

Measure water and honey into a large pot, stir well and bring to a boil while you form the bagels.

Roll each lump of dough into a thick "snake" and secure the ends together. Once you have all of your bagels formed, stir honey water and turn the heat down, allowing water to simmer rather than boil. 2 or 3 at a time, drop your bagels into the simmering water, allow to cook for 1 minute, then flip each and allow to cook for another minute. Drain well, place on a parchment lined baking sheet.

Whisk remaining egg together with 1 Tbsp of water, brush over the tops and sides of each bagel, sprinkle generously with choice of seeds. Bake for 15-20 minutes, until golden brown.

* Malt extract powder can be purchased at home brewing supply stores. Do NOT substitute liquid malt extract.

For Gluten-free: I have not yet managed to come up with a gluten-free recipe that is good enough to share.

Paska

Growing up, my absolute favourite part of Easter was this Ukrainian bread, called Paska. My grandmother's neighbor would bake it every year and share it with us. After the egg hunt was over, I knew we'd be going to my grandmother's house and this delicious, citrussy bread would be waiting for us. SO GOOD. It's sweet, almost like a cross between a cake and a bread, and she used to bake it in coffee cans. It's traditionally served at Ukrainian Easter celebrations, and I think of it as a breakfast bread.

Once I grew up and moved out, I had to beg my grandmother to get the recipe for me, which she did. It's always interesting when you're trying to get a recipe through a game of telephone – especially when the first two passes are through old ladies! As usual with my grandmother, the recipe came as more of a formula – no instructions. It was a bit of work to form it into a modern recipe - increasing the flour and zest, changing lard to butter, ditching the coffee can in favour of decorated style, figuring out what the directions would be - but it's been our yearly treat ever since.

I prefer this bread served warm, either fresh out of the oven or microwaved. It's a very tender, moist bread, so be sure to keep it from drying out. Also, it makes a TON of bread, so be prepared to make some friends VERY happy. There seem to be some wildly different ideas of what Paska entails – many don't have citrus, some have a frosting – but this is what I was raised on in Winnipeg, and it won't disappoint!

Warm water	½ cup	125 ml
Granulated sugar	1 tsp	5 ml
Active dry yeast	4 ½ tsp	22 ml
Unsalted butter, softened	3/4 cup	175 ml
Granulated sugar	2 cups	250 ml
Large eggs, beaten	8	8
Lemons, juice and zest of	1	1
Orange, juice and zest of	1	1
Salt	1 tsp	5 ml
Scalded milk, cooled	1 ½ cups	375 ml
All purpose flour, divided	12+ cups	3000+ ml
Large egg yolks	2	2
Water	1 Tbsp	15 ml

Stir sugar into warm water. Sprinkle yeast on top of sugar water, gently stir to incorporate. Allow to sit for 10-15 minutes, until bubbly.

In a stand mixer, cream together butter and sugar until fluffy. Add eggs, continue to beat until well incorporated and fluffy once more. Add juices, zest, and salt to the mixture, mix until combined. Add scalded milk, continue to mix until well incorporated and smooth. Add 4 cups of flour, combine well. Add yeast mixture, mix until well incorporated.

If you have a dough hook attachment for your mixer, affix it now.

Slowly add remaining flour until a good, coherent bread dough comes together. It should be only very slightly sticky to the touch – not super sticky, and not really dry.

Turn dough out onto a floured surface, and knead for a few minutes. Dough should be smooth, elastic, and no longer sticky when it's been kneaded enough.

Put dough into a very large, lightly greased bowl or pot - or two - cover top with plastic wrap, and allow to rise in a warm area until doubled in size, about 1 ½ -2 hours. Once doubled, beat down the middle of the dough and allow to rise another hour.

Reserve about 1/3 of the dough for decorations, and divide remaining dough out among the pans you'll be using (grease them first!). For reference, we use a 9" round Pyrex pot, a large loaf pan, and 3 mini loaf pans to bake one batch of Paska.

For the main body of your breads, you'll want the dough to fill about 1/3 of each baking pan – they'll rise like crazy. Halfway full if you're adventurous, but don't say I didn't warn you. Cover bread pans and reserved 1/3 dough loosely with plastic wrap and allow to rise another 30 minutes.

Once your 30 minutes are up, use the reserved dough to make designs on the top of each loaf. Braids, twists, curls, crosses and rosettes are popular/traditional, but have fun with it. (Google can be a great source of design inspiration.) Toothpicks can be used to help secure designs in place until after baking. Cover loosely with plastic, allow to rise one last time, 30 minutes.

While your dough is rising, whisk together the remaining egg yolks and water to create an egg wash. This glaze will give your finished Paska a shiny, dark brown finish. Beautiful!

Preheat oven to 350 F (180 C).

Once final rise is finished, brush entire top of each loaf with egg wash. Bake loaves for 10 minutes. Without opening the oven door, lower the heat to 325 F (160 C) and continue to bake for another 40 minutes.

Cool Paska for 10-15 minutes (if you can handle the wait), then gently remove from pans and transfer to a wire rack or wooden cutting board to continue cooling.

For Gluten-free: I have not yet managed to come up with a gluten-free recipe that is good enough to share.

Paska

Peameal Bacon

Peameal and Back Bacon

In the USA, a very rough equivalent of back bacon is sold as "Canadian Bacon" - but it tends to lack flavour, and is more like basic ham than anything. While sold in stores along with other breakfast style meats, you're most likely to see "Canadian bacon" on pizza. Fun fact, on that note: The meat isn't the only thing Canadian about "Hawaiian" pizza - the pizza itself was invented by a Canadian!

While back bacon sort of has a presence south of our border, peameal bacon does not enjoy any real notoriety outside of Canada, where it was invented in Toronto. Originally coated in ground up dried peas, modern "peameal" bacon is actually coated in cornmeal. It's easier on the teeth!

Anyway, both back bacon and peameal bacon start out the same – as pork loin soaking in a flavourful brine for a few days – and then veer off in different directions from there:

Peameal bacon is then rolled in cornmeal, wrapped, and chilled. It's then cut into thick slices and fried up as needed, usually served in sandwiches. I like my peameal sandwiches with spinach, tomato, red onion, sharp cheddar cheese, and roasted garlic aioli - heaven!

Back bacon, on the other hand, skips the cornmeal, and gets smoked until fully cooked. You can serve it as-is, though it's usually reheated in some form: fried as part of breakfast or in a sandwich, or thinly sliced and used to make pizza. I promise you, making a pizza with this will wreck you for all other "Canadian bacon" pizzas. I make my own spicy version of Hawaiian pizza - back bacon, pineapple, thinly sliced jalapenos, and a drizzle of Sriracha.. spectacular!

While back bacon requires smoking – usually requiring special equipment / technique – peameal bacon is ridiculously easy to make, and requires no special skill or equipment. I like to divide my batch of cured meat, doing half as peameal, and smoke the rest.

Makes about 4 lbs worth of meat

1 Pork loin, about	4 lbs	2 kg
Cold water, divided	12 cups	3 L
Maple syrup	1 cup	250 ml
Pickling salt	½ cup	125 ml
Prague powder #1 cure	2 Tbsp	30 ml
Mustard seeds	2 Tbsp	30 ml
Black peppercorns	2 tsp	10 ml
Garlic cloves, pressed	4	4
Whole cloves	3	3
Bay leaves	2	2
Lemon, sliced into wedges	1	1

Cut pork loin into 2 approximately equal sized chunks (crosswise, NOT lengthwise!). Trim most of the visible fat, if you'd like. Some people don't bother, but I don't like the extra fat on mine. Set chill until ready to use.

Measure 4 cups of water into a large pot, add remaining ingredients, aside from pork and rest of water. Bring to a boil, reduce heat, and simmer for 5 minutes. Remove from heat, add remaining water, stir to combine. Allow to cool to room temperature.

Place one chunk of pork loin in each of 2 gallon sized freezer bags. I like to manually divide the lemon wedges and bay leaves equally between the two bags before pouring half of the brine into each bag. Push out most of the air, seal the bags, and put them in the fridge – I put both bags into a 9 x 12 cake pan, just in case of leakage, etc.

Allow the pork to brine for 5 whole days, turning once daily to ensure the pork loins are completely submerged.

After 5 days, discard brine, and rinse pork loins with cold water. Use paper towels to pat dry.

For Peameal Bacon

Pour a generous amount of yellow cornmeal onto a plate large enough to accommodate the chunk of pork loin. Roll loin in the cornmeal, pressing to form a uniform crust.

Wrap tightly in plastic wrap, chill for at least an hour before slicing and frying/grilling… if you can handle the wait - we usually let impatience get the better of us.

For Back Bacon

Hot smoke with your choice of wood chips until it reaches an internal temperature of 145-150 F. (62.5 - 65.5 C)

Back Bacon

Cretons

Cretons – it's a goofy food name for us Anglos. Looking at it, it looks like someone typoed "Cretin". It's actually pronounced something like "Cret-AWN", and is a hugely popular breakfast food in Quebec.

I first had this when I was in my early teens, visiting my father in Montreal. Hated it! The spiced pork pate looked really gross in the plastic tub it came in, and the idea of putting cinnamon and cloves in a savoury pâté was completely foreign to my barely developed palate. I think the idea of it managed to confuse my actual taste buds at the time, because – as an adult – I love the stuff. I love spreading meat on toast for breakfast – cretons comes second only to my all time favourite breakfast: Haggis on a toasted bagel.

Cretons is a lot easier to come by than haggis, though. It requires no fancy or hard to find ingredients, and whips up fairly quickly at home. This is my version, which is not only gluten free - omitting bread as an ingredient - but a slightly spicier than some of the grocery store cretons I've had in Quebec. This makes a good amount for a family, but feel free to cut the recipe in half if needed.

Makes about 1 ½ lbs

Ground pork	2 lbs	1 kg
Large onion, peeled & finely chopped	1	1
Garlic cloves, pressed or minced	2	2
Cinnamon	½ tsp	2 ml
Ground cloves	½ tsp	2 ml
Allspice	1/4 tsp	1 ml
Ground ginger	1/4 tsp	1 ml
Milk	2 cups	500 ml
Bay leaf	1	1
Dried parsley	1 tsp	5 ml
or		
Dried summer savoury	½ -1 tsp	5-10 ml
Salt and pepper, to taste		

In a large pan, mash together pork, onion, garlic, and spices. Add milk a little at a time, stirring to create a runny paste. Add bay leaf. Cook over medium heat, stirring occasionally, until almost all of the milk is absorbed/cooked off. Remove bay leaf, add parsley or summer savoury, stir well. Season with salt and pepper to taste. Continue cooking until all milk is absorbed / cooked off.

Transfer cretons to a storage dish with a lid, as-is (pictured), or put in the food processor and puree for a finer texture. Chill well, stir before serving for the first time. Store in the fridge for up to a week.

Cretons

Prairie Grain Cereal

I designed this recipe as a gluten-free version of a favourite hot cereal back home, named after the Red River. As the original was made from wheat and rye - along with flax - it was no longer an option for me. Still, I missed the toasty, nutty flavours of it!

This recipe can be made two ways: ground, or whole grain. Both are hearty, high fibre, flavourful ways to start the morning. They're especially great to start off a day spent outside in cold weather - they're filling, and really warm you up from the inside out.

Ground: Quick to cook up, with a porridge texture.

Whole Grain: Having the different sizes and textures of the different grains, is a lot of fun - they all have different flavours, sizes, shapes, and firmness. It gives the bowl an interesting character.

I like to mix up a batch of the grains and store them in an airtight container. This mixture is enough for 10-16 servings.

Flax seeds	1 cup	250 ml
Whole buckwheat	1 cup	250 ml
Whole millet	1 cup	250 ml
Whole sorghum	1 cup	250 ml
Teff grain	½ cup	125 ml
Amaranth	1/4 cup	50 ml

In batches, place grains in a large, dry nonstick pan. Cook over medium heat until fragrant. Remove from heat, mix all toasted grains together, allow to cool.

Ground Cereal: Process grains in a coffee grinder in small batches, until grains are slightly bigger than grains of sand.

To serve, measure 1/3 cup grain mixture per serving into a pot, top with 1 cup of water per serving. Bring to a boil, turn heat down and simmer until water is absorbed into the grains - about 10 minutes.

Whole Grain Cereal: Place half of the toasted, unprocessed grain mixture into a slow cooker. Add 8 cups of water, stir well, and cook on low overnight. (A crust of flax seeds may form, it's all good!). Serves 5-8.

To serve either way:

Season with salt, to taste. Spoon into bowls, and customize to taste: add milk, sugar, brown sugar, maple syrup, raisins, and or chopped nuts.

Prairie Grain Cereal

"Succulent" Potatoes

Appetizers & Sides

"Succulent" Potatoes

The source material for this is named for a plant that doesn't grow naturally in Canada, made by a restaurant named for an American city. While all of that sounds less-than-Canadian, it's an appetizer that is high on the list of "things I have to eat when visiting home!" for many expat Canadians!

You'll want to plan ahead when preparing these - they do best when marinated overnight, and the accompanying dip tastes better after allowing the flavours to meld overnight.

Makes 4-6 servings

Large Yukon gold potatoes	2-3	2-3
Jalapeno juice *	1 ½ cups	375 ml
Oil for frying		
Salt		

Scrub potatoes before thinly slicing - we like to use a mandolin for this. Soak potato slices in hot water for 20 minutes, drain well, pat dry with paper towels. Toss dried potato slices with jalapeno juice, place in a covered container and allow to marinate overnight.

Heat oil to 350 F (180 C). You can use a deep fryer, or a heavy pot. If not using a deep fryer, use a deep, heavy pot, filled to at least 4" deep. In small batches, fry sliced potatoes in preheated oil, until crispy and golden. Transfer to plate lined with paper towels, blot any excess grease before carefully transferring to serving plate. Serve warm, with "Succulent" Dip.

* Jalapeno juice: the brine drained off cans of pickled jalapenos.

"Succulent" Dip

Sour cream	1 cup	250 ml
Creamy Caesar dressing	½ cup	125 ml
Shredded Parmesan cheese	1/4 cup	50 ml
Finely chopped green onion	2-3 Tbsp	30-45 ml
Crushed chilies / red pepper flakes	1/2-1 tsp	2-5 ml

Whisk all ingredients together. Cover, chill until use - ideally overnight.

29

Poutine

Poutine

Poutine is.. well, honestly it's a little nasty, and definitely not a pretty dish. It's a 2 am-going-home-from-the-bar kinda food. There is nothing redeeming in nutrition OR appearance. It's not haute cuisine in the slightest. It may just end up clogging your arteries on sight. Sometimes, I'm kinda embarrassed that it's sort of looked at as our national dish in Canada... not to mention being wholly representative of Canadian cuisine, to non-Canadians! Oh, but it can be soooo good!

Done right, when you're in the right mood for it, it can take the concept of "comfort food" to whole new levels. I'm pretty sure that making it for a boyfriend has a high chance of resulting in a marriage proposal – I know my husband would marry me all over again for poutine. (He actually proposed because I made him a sandwich. No joke – it was a muffaletta.)

Poutine is a pretty simple dish from Quebec, consisting of fries, cheese curds, and "gravy". Sorry, I have to put that in quotes, as I'm a gravy snob. The most popular – and "correct" way of making the sauce, in Canada, is to use a packet mix. I'm vehemently opposed to pretty much any sauce that comes from a powder, so here is how I make it, from scratch. Very much worth it!

A few notes, as I tend to bastardize things up quite a bit to suit my tastes:

-       Traditionally, the sauce is a chicken based velouté sauce. I've *always* preferred a beef based sauce, as I find it has more flavour. Mixing chicken and beef together is a great middle ground. The sauce is something that would make any foodie turn up their nose, but is the closest thing to authentic that you're going to get. I don't want anyone to think that this is the sort of gravy that I turn out for anything other than Poutine. LOL

-       Hint: crumbled bacon and thinly sliced green onions are not traditional, but really go well sprinkled on top of poutine.

-       Cheese curds should be as fresh as humanly possible – a couple days old at max, if at all possible. Freshness and bringing them to room temperature ensures a nice squeak!

-       Traditionally, poutine is made with a very light (blond) roux. Well, I prefer a bit darker roux (more flavour!), which this recipe is based on. The lighter the roux, the more thickening power, so if you want to go lighter, you'll need a bit more broth than this recipe calls for.

-       As with most of my "recipes" at home, I usually don't measure anything. I did measure for the sauce this time around, to give you a base idea of what works.

31

This makes enough sauce for 3-4 servings, feel free to double the recipe as needed. Other ingredients, just eyeball it all, to your tastes.

Russet Potatoes, scrubbed clean		
Cheese curds		
Butter	1/4 cup	50 ml
All-purpose flour	1/4 cup	50 ml
Corn starch	1 Tbsp	15 ml
Beef broth	2 cups	500 ml
Chicken broth	1 cup	250 ml
Garlic cloves, minced or pressed	2	2
Salt and pepper		
Oil for deep frying		

Cut potatoes into french fries, place into a bowl of cold water for about an hour. Remove cheese curds from fridge, allow to come to room temperature as you work on everything else.

In a saucepan, melt the butter over medium-low heat. Add rice flour, corn starch, and pepper, stir well until fully incorporated. Continue to cook, stirring constantly, until flour mixture becomes the colour of peanut butter. This is called a roux, and cooking it to this level will impart a nice, somewhat nutty flavour to the sauce.

Once roux has obtained the right colour, slowly add broth and garlic. It will steam like CRAZY, so be careful. Stir as you go, until sauce is smooth. Taste, season with salt and pepper as needed. Allow to simmer on medium heat for a few minutes, until slightly thickened. This is NOT supposed to be a thick gravy! Once the sauce is a good consistency, remove from heat and set aside.

Heat oil to 325 F (160 C). Remove fries from water, blot dry. In small batches, cook fries for 10 minutes. This will NOT brown them, merely cook them. As each batch comes out, put aside. Once all fries are par-cooked / blanched, turn the heat up to 375 f (190 C), and allow oil to reach temperature. In small batches, re-fry the potatoes until browned and crispy, about 3 minutes per batch.

Yes, it seems a little involved – but this is how to get fries that are cooked all the way through, and crispy on the outside!

To assemble the Poutine:

Mound hot fries on serving plate. Add a handful of cheese curds, stir slightly before smothering with sauce, top with bacon & green onions. Serve immediately... soggy poutine is sad poutine!

For Gluten-Free: Use brown rice flour instead of all-purpose flour

Montreal Smoked Meat

Montreal smoked meat is - as you can tell by the name - a Montreal specialty. That said, it's popular in various other areas of Canada, whether as a locally-made product, or shipped in directly from Montreal. You can buy thinly sliced smoked meat prepacked as deli meat, and - in some places - you can go to a deli and order an amazing sandwich, piled high with thickly sliced smoked meat.

Make no mistake, this is NOT pastrami. The cut of beef used is different, the technique is a bit different, the brine is different, and the rub is specifically Montreal Steak Spice. (Smoked meat came first, then eventually the spices used to make it were marketed as their own thing!)

This is a bit of an undertaking to do - you're dealing with a whole brisket, that you'll trim, cure, soak, smoke, and finally steam. In the end, it's worth it!

1 Whole Brisket with fat trimmed to 1/4"   12-16 lbs   5 ½ - 7 1/4 kg

Cure:

Salt	1 1/4 cup	300 ml
Prague Powder	1 Tbsp	15 ml
Coarse ground black pepper	1/4 cup	50 ml
Ground coriander	2 Tbsp	30 ml
Granulated sugar	1 Tbsp	15 ml
Ground bay leaves	1 Tbsp	15 ml
Ground cloves	1 ½ tsp	7 ml

Rub:

2 batches Montreal Steak Spice, but OMIT THE SALT. (Page 144)

In a large bowl, mix cure ingredients. Rub cure over entire brisket.

Place brisket in a very large plastic bag, seal well, and place in a large container, in fridge. Flip brisket at least once - ideally twice - per day, for 10 days.

On the morning of the 11th day, thoroughly rinse the brisket off, before soaking in clean water for 3 hours, changing the water every 30 minutes. Once soaking is done, pat dry with paper towels. Coat entire brisket with Montreal Steak Spice - again, omit the salt! This is important.

Hot smoke the with your choice of wood chips (We like applewood or maple for this) at 225 F (107 C), fat size up, until it reaches an internal temperature of 165 F (74 C). This will take about 7-8 hours.

Set up a large roasting pan with a V rack (like you'd use to roast a turkey). Add an inch or two of water to the pan, before placing the smoked brisket in the rack. Tightly cover top of pan with foil, set pan to span two burners on your stove top, if it fits.

Bring water to a boil over high heat, reduce to medium-low and simmer for 3 hours. Listen well - you want the water to keep at a nice simmer, without being a rolling boil, the whole time. As water vapourizes, add more hot water to keep it going.

As you near the 3 hour mark, insert a meat thermometer into the thickest spot. You'll want the meat to reach 180 F (82 C). Carefully re-foil the whole thing, trying seal steam in.

Once the meat reaches the proper temperature, remove from heat, and allow to rest for 10 minutes.

Slice rested meat as thinly or thickly as you like.

Best served as a sandwich with rye bread (try the Winnipeg style rye, page 46!), with plenty of mustard.

Chill any leftover meat, eat within a week or so.

If you'd like to freeze a portion of smoked meat, wrap tightly in plastic wrap before placing in a freezer bag and vacuum sealing it. If you do not have a vacuum sealer, be sure to squeeze out as much air as possible.

Freeze for up to 3 months.

Montreal Smoked Meat

Cream Cheese Dips

Cream Cheese Dips

There is a line of cream cheese dips back home that is very popular, but not really seen as a Canadian thing... until you leave. Amazingly enough, while the brand that produces them is widely available in the US, this particular product is not carried anywhere but in Canada.

I've created replicas for all 6 flavours. From the top down on the photo to the left, you see Jalapeno, Onion, and French Onion. From the top down on the page 39 photo, you see Dill Pickle, Herb & Garlic, and Herb & Spice.

Jalapeno Cream Cheese Dip

Makes about 2 cups

Medium red bell pepper	1	1
Jalapeno peppers	1-2	1-2
Milk	1 cup	250 ml
Cream cheese, softened	8 oz	250 g
White vinegar	2 Tbsp	30 ml
Corn starch	2 tsp	10 ml
Salt	1/4-1/2 tsp	1-2 ml

Seed and finely chop / puree peppers, place in a small saucepan, along with milk. Bring peppers and milk to a boil, turn heat down, simmer 10 minutes. Remove from heat, allow to cool, strain steeped milk into another pot.

Add cream cheese, vinegar, corn starch, and salt, to taste. Whisk until smooth and well combined. Bring to a simmer over medium heat, stirring constantly until thickened. Remove from heat, cool to room temperature before covering and chilling until cold

Onion Cream Cheese Dip

Makes about 2 cups

Milk	1 cup	250 ml
Packet onion soup mix powder (1 oz)	1	1
Corn starch	2 tsp	10 ml
Cream cheese, softened	8 oz	250 g

In a small saucepan, whisk together milk, onion soup mix, and corn starch. Add cream cheese, whisk until smooth. Bring to a simmer over medium heat, stirring constantly until thickened.
Remove from heat, cool to room temperature before covering and chilling until cold.

French Onion Cream Cheese Dip

Makes about 2 cups

Milk	1 cup	250 ml
Corn starch	2 tsp	10 ml
Cream cheese, softened	8 oz	250 g
Dried onion flakes	2 Tbsp	30 ml
Dried chives	1 tsp	5 ml
Onion powder	½ tsp	2 ml
Seasoned salt	½ tsp	2 ml
Salt	1/4 tsp	1 ml

In a small saucepan, whisk together milk and corn starch. Add cream cheese, whisk until smooth. Add remaining ingredients, whisk until well combined.

Bring to a simmer over medium heat, stirring constantly until thickened.

Remove from heat, cool to room temperature before covering and chilling until cold.

Dill Pickle Cream Cheese Dip

Makes about 2 ½ cups

Milk	3/4 cup	175 ml
Pickle brine	1/4 cup	50 ml
Corn starch	2 tsp	10 ml
Cream cheese, softened	8 oz	250 g
Finely chopped dill pickles	3/4 cup	175 ml
Salt	1/4 tsp	1 ml

In a small saucepan, whisk together milk, pickle brine, and corn starch. Add cream cheese, whisk until smooth. Add chopped pickles and salt, stir to combine.

Bring to a simmer over medium heat, stirring constantly until thickened.

Remove from heat, cool to room temperature before covering and chilling until cold.

Cream Cheese Dips

Herb & Garlic Cream Cheese Dip

Makes about 2 cups

Milk	1 cup	250 ml
Corn starch	2 tsp	10 ml
Cream cheese, softened	8 oz	250 g
Dried onion flakes	1 Tbsp	15 ml
Garlic powder	1 1/4 tsp	6 ml
Dried chives	1 tsp	5 ml
Dried parsley	½ tsp	2 ml
Salt	½ tsp	2 ml
White vinegar	½ tsp	2 ml
Seasoned salt	1/4 tsp	1 ml

In a small saucepan, whisk together milk and corn starch. Add cream cheese, whisk until smooth. Add remaining ingredients, whisk until well combined. Bring to a simmer over medium heat, stirring constantly until thickened.

Remove from heat, cool to room temperature before covering and chilling until cold.

Herb & Spice Cream Cheese Dip

Makes about 2 cups

Milk	1 cup	250 ml
Corn starch	2 tsp	10 ml
Cream cheese, softened	8 oz	250 g
Dried onions	1 Tbsp	15 ml
Garlic powder	1 tsp	5 ml
Chili powder	½ tsp	2 ml
Dried chives	½ tsp	2 ml
Salt	½ tsp	2 ml
White vinegar	½ tsp	2 ml
Dried parsley	1/4 tsp	1 ml
Seasoned salt	1/4 tsp	1 ml

In a small saucepan, whisk together milk and corn starch. Add cream cheese, whisk until smooth. Add remaining ingredients, whisk until well combined.

Bring to a simmer over medium heat, stirring constantly until thickened.

Remove from heat, cool to room temperature before covering and chilling until cold.

Meat Paste Egg Rolls

Egg rolls are a funny thing in Canada - they vary wildly based on region. In most places, they're wrapped the way described here, rather than the burrito-style wrapping that is common elsewhere.

In Ottawa, they're cylindrical and mostly meat. One end is left open, and the meat spilling out gets very brown - those "burnt end" eggrolls are hugely popular!

In Halifax, it's all about the meat paste egg rolls. Sure, there's a small amount of vegetable matter in there... but it's dwarfed and enveloped by the star of the show - meat!

One could probably write a whole chapter on the various styles of egg rolls, but for the purposes of this book, I'm going with the most requested style from my readers - the meat paste egg roll.

Makes about 10 egg rolls

Vegetable, canola, or peanut oil, for frying.		
Butter	1 Tbsp	15 ml
Small onion, finely chopped	1	1
Shredded cabbage	3/4 cup	175 ml
Celery stalk, finely chopped	1	1
Salt		
Ground pork	1 lb	500 g
Garlic cloves, pressed or minced	2	2
Sesame oil	2 tsp	10 ml
Grated ginger	1 tsp	5 ml
Crushed chilies / red pepper flakes	1/4 tsp	1 ml
Green onions, chopped	2	2
Ground black pepper, to taste		

10 egg roll wrappers
Plum sauce (Page 136)

Heat oil to 375 F (190 C). You can use a deep fryer, or a heavy pot. If not using a deep fryer, use a deep, heavy pot, filled to at least 4" deep.

In a large pan, melt butter. Add onion, cabbage, and celery, sprinkle with a little salt and saute until tender. Add ground pork, garlic, sesame oil, ginger, and chilies, stirring occasionally until pork is browned and cooked through, and liquid has all cooked off.

Transfer pork mixture to a food processor, along with green onions, and blitz until very smooth. Season with salt and pepper to taste.

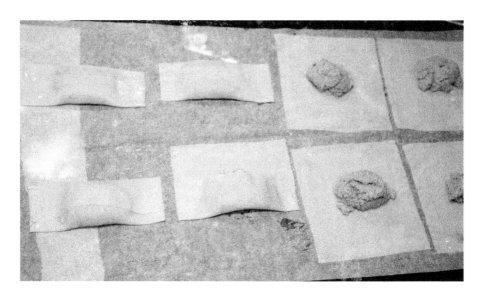

Lay out an egg roll wrapper on your workspace. Using a pastry brush (or just your fingers!), brush a bit of water around the entire edge of the wrapper – about a 1" border. Measure about 1/4 cup of filling in the center of the wrapper.

Fold one side of the wrapper across the filling, to about 2/3 of the way across the wrapper. Fold the other side of the wrapper across the first side, effectively folding the sheet into thirds, while enclosing the filing.

Gently squeezing air out as you work, press firmly down on all edges, to seal. Repeat for remaining filling / wrappers.

Carefully place egg rolls - seam side down - in preheated oil. Fry, turning occasionally, until crispy and golden. Transfer to plate lined with paper towels, blot any excess grease before carefully transferring to serving plate.

Serve hot, with plum sauce

Variation: Baked Egg Rolls

Line a baking sheet with parchment paper, spray with nonstick cooking spray. Arrange egg rolls - seam side down - on baking sheet, brush with oil.

Bake for 10 minutes at 375 F (190 C). Flip egg rolls over, bake for another 10 minutes, or until crispy and golden.

For Gluten-free: Use pre-made gluten-free egg roll wrappers, or your favourite gluten-free egg roll wrapper / wonton recipe.

Meat Paste Egg Rolls

Green Onion Cake

Green Onion Cakes are VERY much an Edmonton thing - there's even a campaign on the go, looking to designate them Edmonton's Official Food. You can find them in many Asian restaurants, in some grocers, and at festivals, served out of food trucks. There are entire food trucks dedicated to green onion cakes, serving them up plain, "taco style" with various fillings, and with various choices in dipping sauce.

All-purple flour	3 cups	750 ml
Baking powder	1 Tbsp	15 ml
Salt	1/4 tsp	1 ml
Baking soda	1/8 tsp	½ ml
Boiling water	1 ½ cup	375 ml
Butter	2 Tbsp	30 ml
Sesame oil	2 Tbsp	30 ml
Salt and pepper		
Green onions	1 cup	250 ml
Vegetable or peanut oil for frying		

In a large bowl - I like to use a stand mixer for this - mix together flour, baking powder, salt, and baking soda. Add boiling water, mixing together to form a soft dough. Knead for about 5 minutes - or use a dough hook in a stand mixer - until dough is soft, elastic, and not sticky. You may need to add a little more water or flour as necessary. Cover dough with plastic wrap and allow to sit, undisturbed, for 30 minutes.

Transfer dough to a clean, floured work surface. Roll into a log shape, divide into 8 equally-sized pieces. Melt butter, whisk together with sesame oil. Roll one dough piece out into a long, thin disk. Brush liberally with sesame-butter mixture. Sprinkle with a little salt and pepper, then with green onion slices.

Starting with the long edge closest to you, tightly roll the disk up, like a cigar. Brush top with oil mix. Starting from one of the ends of the "cigar", coil the dough up into a tight spiral. Press spiral between your hands to flatten out into a disk, 1/4" thick or so, depending on your tastes. Set aside, repeat for remaining dough portions.

Drizzle a couple Tbsp worth of oil into a frying pan, heat over medium. One or two at a time, fry an onion cake for about 4 minutes, or until nicely golden brown underneath. Flip once, fry for another 3 or so minutes, until both sides are golden brown. Keep an eye on it - you don't want them to burn!

Once cooked, transfer to a plate lined with paper towels. Use an additional paper towel to blot excess oil. Serve hot, with Sambal Oelek sauce, sriracha, plum sauce, and/or soy sauce for dipping.

For Gluten-free: Omit all purpose flour. Add 1 ½ cups light buckwheat flour, 1 cup sweet rice flour, 2 Tbsp corn starch, and 1 tsp xanthan gum.

Green Onion Cakes

Winnipeg Style Rye Bread

In many areas of Canada, "rye" bread tends to have no seeds. In Winnipeg, that deviation from the "rye" norm goes a bit further - rye bread doesn't actually use rye flour!

Winnipeg rye is basically a white bread that is liberally studded with little bits of cracked rye kernels, making for a softer, fluffier bread - perfect for sandwiches! This bread works spectacularly with Montreal Smoked Meat, page 33.

Cracked rye	½ cup	125 ml
Hot water	½ cup	125 ml
Active dry yeast	2 tsp	10 ml
Brown sugar, packed	1 Tbsp	15 ml
Warm - not hot -water	3/4 cup	175 ml
All-purpose flour	4 1/4 cups	1050 ml
Salt	2 tsp	10 ml
Milk, warmed to lukewarm	3/4 cup	175 ml
Vegetable oil	3 Tbsp	45 ml
Large egg	1	1
Cornmeal (optional)		
Large egg	1	1
Milk	1 Tbsp	15 ml

Mix together rye and hot water in a small bowl or mug. Cover, allow to soak over night.

The next day, stir yeast and brown sugar into warm water, allow to stand for 10 minutes – it should get very bubbly.

In a large mixing bowl, combine flour, salt, and soaked rye. Pour in yeast mixture, warm milk, oil, and egg, stir well to combine. Dump dough out onto a floured surface, knead until soft and elastic, 5-10 minutes. (OR: mix it in a stand mixer with a dough hook for 5 minutes or so!). Once dough is fully kneaded, place in a greased bowl, cover with plastic wrap, and allow to rise in a warm place for one hour, or until doubled in size.

Divide dough into two equal sized balls, form into oblong or round loaves. Place loaves on a parchment lined baking sheet (you can scatter corn meal on the paper first, if you like), cover loosely with plastic wrap and allow to rise for another hour.

Preheat oven to 350 F (180 C). Whisk together remaining egg and milk, brush over the loaves. Using a sharp knife, cut a few 1" deep slashes in the top of each loaf. Bake for 35-40 minutes, or until golden brown.

For Gluten-free: As rye itself is a source of gluten, this cannot be made gluten-free

Winnipeg Style Rye Bread

Hodge Podge

Hodge podge is a one-pot vegetable dish from Nova Scotia. Not really a soup, not really a stew, it's cheap, easy to make, and VERY adaptable. There are many arguments over what is "right", and whose grandma makes it the best. You can follow this recipe as-is, or swap out whatever happens to be growing in your yard at the time.

Beans - green and/or yellow - carrots, and potatoes are pretty well standard, with other veggies being added as desired/available. Some prefer to use shelled peas - I like the crunch, so I leave them whole. Some people prefer to cook all the vegetables together, but I find that the more delicate ones get overcooked this way - I prefer to cook in stages, much like Jiggs Dinner (Page 115). No matter how you like it, Hodge Podge is something that doesn't usually turn out exactly the same thing, twice!

While this is a simple dish, it's mind-blowingly good when done with the newest, freshest vegetables. It's the reason Nova Scotians anxiously await the first potatoes, carrots, and beans of the season! Serve this with some nice crusty bread for dunking.

Serves 4 as a dinner, 6 or so as a side.

New potatoes	1-2 lbs	500-1000 g
New carrots	1-2 lbs	500-1000 g
Green beans	1 cup	250 ml
Yellow beans	1 cup	250 ml
Fresh peas	1 cup	250 ml
Butter	½ cup	125 ml
Heavy cream	1 cup	250 ml
Milk	½ cup	125 ml
Salt and pepper		

Wash all vegetables. Cut the potatoes in half - large potatoes can be quartered. Aim to have the pieces all basically the same size. Cut the ends off the carrots. Cut into bite sized chunks, or split in half lengthwise (looks pretty!). Cut the ends off the beans.

Get a pot of water boiling, add a little salt. Add potatoes to water, bring back to a boil, allow to cook for 5 minutes. If your carrots are in chunks, add after the potatoes have been cooking for 5 minutes. If they're split in half lengthwise, allow the potatoes to cook for 10 minutes before adding them. Allow carrots to cook for 5 minutes, then add the beans. Cook for another 5 minutes. Add the peas, cook for another 2 minutes.

Strain off the vegetables, reserving ½ cup of the pot water. Return the reserved cup of liquid to the pot, alone with the butter, heavy cream, and milk. Whisk well to combine, and season with salt and pepper - to taste - before returning vegetables to the pot. Allow the whole thing to cook for another 5 minutes or so. Taste, adjust salt and pepper if desired. Serve immediately.

Hodge Podge

"Work Boot" Candy

Snack Foods

"Work Boot" Candy

This recipe is based on a mass produced candy, originally produced out of my hometown. One Winnipegger wanted to market his grandmother's candy, got together with a childhood friend of his, and got to work. Within a few years, the candy was selling all over Canada.

This is one of those recipes that is so minimalist in both ingredients and preparation, I'm a little embarrassed to publish it. This has only 3 simple ingredients – white chocolate, cashews, and graham crackers – and it whips up in no time. Have bowls of this out at holiday parties, or package them up for a hostess gift, stocking stuffer, or "Thank you" that your friends and family will love!

Be sure to use actual white chocolate chips for this, not "melting candy" disks.

Makes about 1 ½ lbs / 750 g of candy

Graham crackers	1 sleeve	1 sleeve
Salted cashew pieces	1 cup	250 ml
Bag GOOD white chocolate chips	11 oz	312 g

Prepare a baking sheet or other flat surface with a large piece of parchment paper.

Smash up about a sleeve worth of graham crackers, into bite sized pieces. Measure two cups of the graham bits into a large bowl. I measured out chunks AND the fine particles, which makes the candy as shown. For a "prettier" candy, don't include the fine particles in your measurement. Add cashews, stir lightly to distribute.

In a microwave safe bowl, melt chocolate chips – I usually do 45 second increments, stirring in between each.

When chocolate is fully melted, pour over graham/cashew mixture, stir well to coat everything. Turn mixture out onto parchment paper, spreading mixture out to form bite sized chunks.

Cool until set, break up any really large pieces. Store in airtight bags / containers.

For Gluten-free: Use gluten-free graham crackers. (I have a great recipe in Beyond Flour 2!)

Cape Breton Oat Cakes

This is one of those instances where a Canadian recipe is kind of a bastardized version of an immigrant recipe. These are a sweetened version of the Scottish oatcake. Rather than being served alongside savoury foods, or as a kind of cracker, these are served as a kind of tea biscuit, or cookie.

Some people like these thicker and slightly chewier, some prefer thin and very crispy. Some like them as round cookies, some like rectangles or squares, and others like to cut them first into squares, and then into triangles. Do whatever feels good to you!

Makes about 24 2 ½ " square biscuits

All-purpose flour	2 cups	500 ml
Rolled oats	2 cups	500 ml
Brown sugar, packed	½ cup	125 ml
Granulated sugar	½ cup	125 ml
Baking soda	1 tsp	5 ml
Salt	3/4 tsp	3 ml
Baking powder	½ tsp	2 ml
Butter	½ cup	125 ml
Shortening	½ cup	125 ml
Cold water	½ cup	125 ml

Preheat oven to 350 F (180 C). Line a couple of baking sheets with parchment paper.

In a large mixing bowl, combine dry ingredients. Measure butter and shortening into the same bowl, and cut into the dry ingredients using a pastry cutter or fork. The idea is to work it in until it's evenly distributed throughout, in very small pieces. Add water, stir just until dough comes together. Don't over stir or beat it. If dough is too crumbly, add a small amount of extra water. If the dough is sticky, add a small amount of flour.

Pull dough together into a ball, place on a lightly floured work surface. Gently roll dough out to about 1/4 - ½ " thick, and cut into rounds, squares, rectangles, or triangles, depending on your preference.

Gently arrange oatcakes on prepared baking sheets, leaving 2" between biscuits. Bake for 12-15 minutes, or until golden brown on top. Remove from oven, allow to cool for a few minutes before gently transferring them to a cooling rack. Once cool, store in an airtight container to keep them crunchy.

For Gluten-free: Mix together 3/4 cup light buckwheat flour, ½ cup oat flour, 1/3 cup sorghum flour, 1/4 cup coconut flour, and 3/4 tsp xanthan gum. Use in place of all-purpose flour. Make sure to use gluten-free certified oats and oat flour.

Cape Breton Oat Cakes

53

Maple Snow Taffy

Maple snow taffy - or "tire d'érable" / "tire sur la neige" in French Canadian areas - is a wintertime treat in maple producing areas of the country. It can be done out in the woods as part of syrup season - in sugar shacks / "cabane à sucre" - or at home. Growing up in Winnipeg, it was very much a Festival Du Voyageur thing. We'd pour boiled maple syrup over packed snow, as we learned about French Canadian culture.

You can make this straight from sap, if you have access, or you can make it with commercially available maple syrup. Just make sure you use actual maple syrup, not pancake syrup. This is a simple, one ingredient recipe, but you do need a few other items to make this:

Large pans
Clean snow
Maple syrup
Glass measuring cup
Popsicle sticks

Pack CLEAN snow into large rectangular cake pans. Set in the freezer, or leave outside - just make sure your clean snow isn't left somewhere that it can get soiled as you prepare your maple syrup!

In a large pot, bring some maple syrup to a boil over medium heat. I'll usually use a cup or so of syrup for 4-ish people, more for a crowd. Affix a candy thermometer and allow to boil until it reaches 240 F (115 C). Remove from heat, transfer to a glass measuring cup.

Pour boiled maple syrup over the snow, in thin lines. Allow to set for a few seconds, affix a popsicle stick to one end, and quickly roll the line of maple syrup onto the stick. Eat immediately, as they will melt!

Maple Snow Taffy

Large Aquatic Rodent Appendages

These pastries are based on a well known, extremely popular pastry, widely available at festivals and fairs across Canada. Dough is stretched out to long ovals and fried, then topped with a variety of goodies. You can go as basic as a brushing of melted butter and sprinkle of cinnamon sugar, or go more wild.

On the "more wild" end, the pastries are usually spread with something sweet - Nutella, peanut butter, Jam, Maple butter, etc - before being sprinkled with candies, chopped nuts, sliced fruits, etc. You can even follow up with a drizzle of more sugar - chocolate sauce, caramel, etc!

Makes 6 pastries

Warm milk	3/4 cup	175 ml
Brown sugar, packed	1/3 cup	75 ml
Active dry yeast	2 ½ tsp	12 ml
Whole wheat flour	2 cups	500 ml
All-purpose flour	½ cup	125 ml
Salt	3/4 tsp	3 ml
Canola oil	2 Tbsp	30 ml
Large egg	1	1
Vanilla extract	1 tsp	5 ml
Canola oil		
Toppings (See next page)		

Combine warm milk with brown sugar, stir until sugar is almost dissolved. Add yeast, stirring until incorporated. Set aside in a warm place for 10 minutes, or until foamy.

In a large bowl, combine flours and salt. Add canola oil, stirring until well distributed. Pour in yeast/milk mixture, egg, and vanilla extract; stir until well combined. Turn dough out onto a clean surface, knead for a few minutes until soft, smooth and elastic. (Alternately, you can "knead" the dough in a stand mixer, using a dough hook)

Pour about 1 Tbsp of canola oil into a large, clean metal or glass bowl. Add freshly kneaded dough to the bowl, turning to coat with the oil. Cover with plastic wrap, set aside in a warm spot to rise for an hour or two, until doubled in size. Once the dough has doubled in size, punch dough down, allow to rise for another 45 minutes.

In a large, deep pot, heat 2-3" of canola oil to 350 F (180 C). While oil is heating, divide dough into 6 equal sized pieces, roll or stretch each out into a long oval, about 1/4" thick. Allow each to rest on a clean work surface as you stretch the rest. Working with one pastry at a time, gently give one final stretch before carefully transferring to the oil. Allow to fry for 1-2 minutes , or until golden on the underside. Gently flip and repeat, cooking until evenly golden.

Transfer fried pastry to a baking sheet lined with paper towels, blot to remove excess oil. Spread and top as desired, serve immediately!

Topping Suggestions:

Cinnamon Sugar: Mix together 1 cup sugar, 1 Tbsp cinnamon. Brush hot pastry with melted butter, sprinkle generously with cinnamon sugar. Squeeze fresh lemon slices on top for a traditional variation on this!

Spreads: Peanut butter, Nutella, maple butter, frosting, jam, pie filling, etc

Toppings: Small candies, crushed chocolate bars, crumbled cookies, sliced fruit, berries, chopped nuts, mini marshmallows, etc

Drizzles: Maple syrup, chocolate sauce, caramel sauce, etc

For Gluten- free: Omit all-purpose and whole wheat flours. Mix together 3/4 cup light buckwheat flour, ½ cup rice bran, ½ cup unflavoured whey protein powder, ½ cup sweet rice flour, 2 Tbsp flax meal, and 2 tsp Xanthan gum, use in place of the removed flours. Mix will be more wet than a normal batch - use moistened hands to shape the dough.

Large Aquatic Rodent Appendages

Sponge Toffee Bars

This is a chocolate coated sponge toffee, and has been a favourite of mine since I was a young kid. Widely available as a candy bar back home, these are pretty easy to make at home.

Beating the hot toffee until it stops actively bubbling is key to getting fine bubbles. If you don't beat the mixture enough, you will get huge, puffy bubbles.. and your slab of toffee will be extremely prone to shattering. Additionally, scoring and re-scoring the slab while it's still warm is also key to it not breaking apart. Not to worry, though: If you toffee breaks and you end up with nuggets instead of pristine bars... it still tastes just as good!

Granulated sugar	2 ½ cups	625 ml
Corn syrup	2/3 cup	150 ml
Water	6 Tbsp	90 ml
Baking soda	1 Tbsp	15 ml
Vanilla extract	2 tsp	10 ml
Dipping Chocolate, page 67		

Prepare a 9" x 13" cake pan with nonstick spray, or a light coating of vegetable oil or shortening. Set aside.

In a LARGE pot, stir together sugar, corn syrup, and water. Attach a candy thermometer to the pan, making sure that it does not touch the bottom of the pan. Bring mixture to a boil, and allow to cook until temperature reaches 300 F (150 C). From the time mixture starts boiling to the time it reaches 300F, do not stir.

Once mixture reaches temperature, remove from heat. Add baking soda and vanilla, beating to incorporate. The mixture will start foaming quite a bit when you add the baking soda, so using a LONG wooden spoon is a good idea. Be very careful - don't burn yourself - but work FAST. Continue beating the mixture until the foaming starts to slow down. Dump foaming mixture into greased cake pan, spreading it out as evenly as possible. Allow it to cool for 15-20 minutes.

When the sponge toffee is starting to harden – but is still quite warm – use a serrated knife to score lines, about 1/4"- ½ " deep in the warm candy. These will be the shapes of your candy bars – I like to make them about 1.25" x 3", or so. Keep in mind that this is not an exact science, and you WILL have breakage in there.

20 minutes later, go back and re-score the lines you already made, gently cutting a little deeper than last time. Allow to cool completely.

Once toffee is cooled all the way through, remove from pan and gently snap along your score lines. If you don't plan to dip them right away, be sure to store toffee in an airtight container – the sugar will attract water from the air, and the toffee can go soggy.

Make up a batch of Dipping Chocolate, page 67. Carefully dip each bar into chocolate, allow excess to drop off, and transfer back to parchment paper. Allow to set completely, before transferring to covered storage container.

Sponge Toffee Bars

Chocolate Peanut Caramel Bars

This recipe is based on a popular candy bar back home. So good, you just want to eat more and more of it!

Temperature is very important on this one, so be sure your candy thermometer is calibrated - you don't want to overcook it! While going a few degrees over temperature for this won't harm the quality or taste, it'll make it more firm and brittle - not the chewy texture we're aiming for!

Light brown sugar, firmly packed	2 cups	500 ml
Sweetened condensed milk	14 oz	396 g
Corn syrup	1 cup	250 ml
Butter	1 cup	250 ml
Salt	1/4 tsp	1 tsp
Vanilla extract	1 ½ tsp	7 ml
Unsweetened baking chocolate, chopped	5 oz	140 g
Roasted unsalted peanuts, finely chopped	1 lb	500 g

Line a baking sheet with parchment paper, spray with cooking spray.

In a large saucepan, combine everything except the vanilla extract, chocolate, and peanuts.

Bring to a boil over medium heat, stirring constantly. Once boiling, affix a candy thermometer to the pan. Make sure the tip of the thermometer is in the sugar mixture, but not touching the bottom of the pan. Boil - stirring constantly - until mixture reaches 235 F (112 C).

Once mixture reaches temperature, immediately remove from heat. Add chocolate and vanilla, stir until chocolate is melted and well combined. Add peanuts, mix until evenly distributed.

Pour onto prepared baking sheet, do your best to spread it out in a thin, even layer. (Spraying the top with nonstick spray, laying a sheet of parchment on top, and then using another baking pan to flatten it is what I like to do!)

Cool to room temperature, before cutting into long, candy bar sized strips - about 1.25" x 7". Wrap each piece with waxed paper or parchment paper, and store in an airtight container.

Note: I find it helpful to spray the knife with cooking spray before I start cutting, and then again every once in a while as I cut.

Chocolate Peanut Caramel Bars

"Wonderful" Crispy Peanut Butter Caramel Bars

To make these gluten-free, just be sure to use gluten-free crispy rice cereal.
Filling:

Creamy peanut butter	1 cup	250 ml
Vanilla extract	½ tsp	2 ml
Salt	½ tsp	2 ml
Crisp rice cereal	2 ½ cups	625 ml
Icing (powdered/confectioner) sugar	1 ½ cups	375 ml

In a stand mixer, beat peanut butter, vanilla extract, and salt together until smooth and well combined. Add cereal, beat well, until cereal is broken up and fully incorporated. Add powdered sugar, beat on low until sugar is completely mixed in.

With clean hands, knead mixture slightly to bring together. Divide into 8 equal sized balls, roll into logs about 3/4" in diameter. Freeze, while you prepare the dipping caramel:

Dipping Caramel

Light brown sugar, firmly packed	2 cups	500 ml
Sweetened condensed milk	14 oz	396 g
Butter	1 cup	250 ml
Corn syrup	1 cup	250 ml
Salt	1/4 tsp	1 ml
Vanilla extract	1 ½ tsp	7 ml

In a large saucepan, combine everything except the vanilla extract. Bring to a boil over medium heat, stirring constantly. Once boiling, affix a candy thermometer to the pan. Make sure the tip of the thermometer is in the sugar mixture, but not touching the bottom of the pan. Boil - stirring constantly - until mixture reaches 240 F (115 C).

Once mixture reaches 240F (115 C), remove from heat and set aside. Allow to cool for 5 minutes, before dipping anything in it.

To Assemble:

Line a baking sheet or flat work area with parchment paper. Carefully dip your frozen filling logs into the warm dipping caramel. Allow excess to drip off, before transferring to parchment paper. Allow to cool and fully set.

Make up a batch of Dipping Chocolate, page 67. Carefully dip each bar into chocolate, allow excess to drop off, and transfer back to parchment paper. Allow to set before transferring to covered storage container.

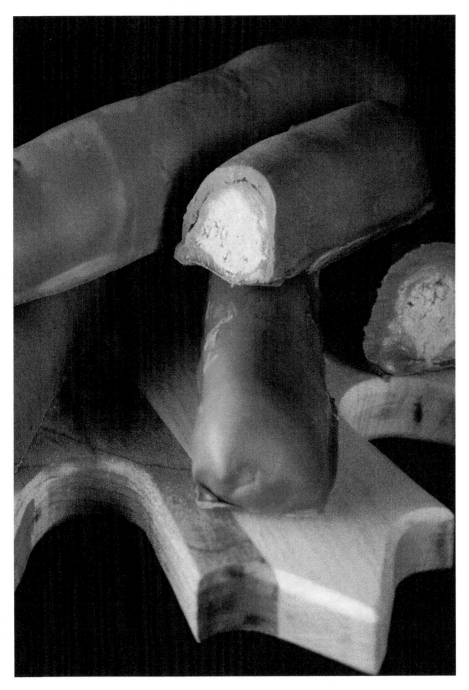

"Wonderful" Crispy Peanut Butter Caramel Bars

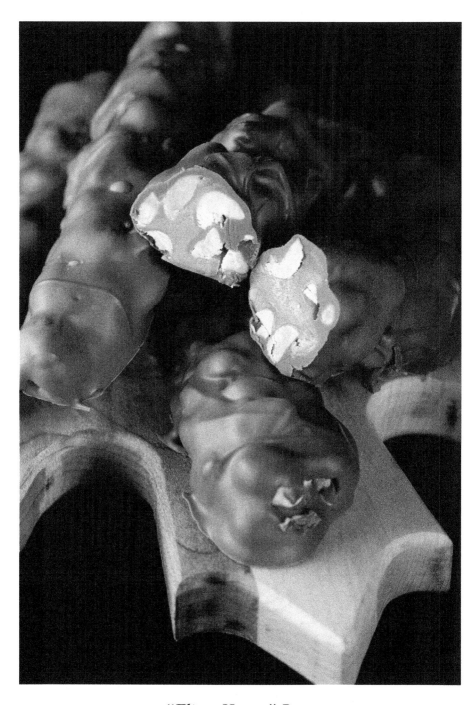

"Flirty Henry" Bars

"Flirty Henry" Bars

Apparently these actually originated in the USA, and you can apparently buy an American version of these in some places, though it's reportedly "not the same thing".

The fudge filling of this recipe makes enough to make a ton of bars - it's just easiest that way, and less likely to burn. Super tasty on its own, you won't have any problem using it up!

Brown sugar, packed	1 ½ cups	375 ml
Granulated sugar	1 ½ cups	375 ml
Heavy cream	1 ½ cup	375 ml
Corn syrup	2/3 cup	150 ml
Butter	1/4 cup	50 ml
Salt	½ tsp	2 ml
Smooth peanut butter	2 Tbsp	30 ml
Vanilla extract	1 tsp	2 ml
Dipping Caramel, page 62		
Roasted peanuts	1 lb	500 g
Dipping Chocolate, page 67		

Spray 9 x 13"pan with nonstick spray, line with parchment paper, spray again. Set aside

In a large saucepan, combine everything up to and including the salt. Bring to a boil over medium heat, stirring until everything is smooth and melted/dissolved together. Once boiling, affix a candy thermometer to the pan. Make sure the tip of the thermometer is in the sugar mixture, but not touching the bottom of the pan. Simmer - without stirring - until mixture reaches 240 F (115 C). Remove from heat.

Add peanut butter and vanilla, carefully beat the sugar mixture until it thickens and loses its shine - you'll see it start to crust on the sides of the saucepan. Pour into the prepared pan, allow cool almost to room temperature.

Slice lengthwise into ½" wide strips, cut each strip into 4" lengths. Carefully remove from pan, transfer to a baking sheet lined with parchment. If desired, roll each strip gently in your hands to soften the corners - it just looks more legit if rounded! Transfer baking sheet to fridge, chill until fully set.

Carefully dip each fudge log into warm - not hot - Dipping Caramel, roll in roasted peanuts, squeezing to set the peanuts in the caramel. Transfer to parchment lined baking sheet, allow to cool before dipping in prepared Dipping Chocolate.

Transfer chocolate dipped bars back to parchment paper to fully set, before transferring to an airtight container for storage.

Chocolate Covered Turkish Delight Bars

Dipping Chocolate

Milk chocolate chips (2 bags)	24 oz	680 g
Shortening	2 Tbsp+	30 ml+

Either in the top of a double boiler - or in a glass bowl, microwaved for 30 seconds at a time - carefully melt chocolate and shortening together, stirring well until smooth.

If chocolate is too thick for dipping, add a little more shortening, once again stirring well until smooth.

Keep chocolate warm while dipping, as it thickens as it cools. Make more as needed.

Chocolate Covered Turkish Delight Bars

I'll admit - I'm not a fan of the source material here. I always assumed it to be an acquired taste - as you hear that Turkish delight is - but I actually like Turkish delight!

To throw another wrench at that assumption, my American husband had never even heard of them before we met as adults, and he LOVES them. Ah, well.

Anyway, The filling on these was a bit challenging to nail down. I'd always assumed it to be a rose flavoured filling, as is popular in Turkish delight... while others described it as "fruity". After a fair amount of experimentation, I nailed it! As it turns out, it's a combination of rose and raspberry.

Turkish delight is notoriously annoying to make, and the center filling for these bars is no exception to that. Be prepared that you may need to make multiple attempts and practice at it, before it turns out perfectly! Just keep a close eye on temperature - overcooking will make it hard

Granulated sugar	4 cups	1000 ml
Water, divided	4 cups	1000 ml
Lemon juice	2 tsp	10 ml
Cream of tartar	1 tsp	5 ml
Cornstarch	1 1/3 cup	325 ml
Rose water	2 tsp	10 ml
LorAnn raspberry flavour oil	½ tsp	2 ml
Magenta food colouring		

Dipping chocolate, above

Spray 9x13" square pan with nonstick spray, line with parchment paper, spray again. Set aside

In a medium sized saucepan, combine sugar, 2 cups of the water, lemon juice, and the cream of tartar. Bring to a boil over medium heat, stirring until the sugar dissolves. Once boiling, reduce heat to medium low and affix a candy thermometer to the pan. Make sure the tip of the thermometer is in the sugar mixture, but not touching the bottom of the pan. Simmer - without stirring - until mixture reaches 260 F (127 C).

While sugar mixture is simmering, measure corn starch into a larger pot. Whisk in remaining 2 cups of water, until no lumps remain. Also, measure your rose water and flavour oil into a small container so that it's ready to go - you won't have a lot of time, when things start to happen!

Once sugar mixture reaches 260 F (127 C), remove from heat. Carefully pour sugar mixture into the larger pot - slowly and a little at a time - whisking each time until smooth.

Cook over medium heat until mixture starts to boil, then reduce heat to medium-low or low. Cook - stirring frequently - until it's ready. The mixture will go from a thinnish liquid, to a thicker liquid, to a thick, glue-like liquid. I like to use a long handled metal spatula for this, so I can really scrape the bottom of the pan as I go.

Eventually, it will act less like a liquid that you need to stir, and more like a more coherent mass that you're pushing around. RIGHT when it starts to come together as more of a coherent mass is when you should remove it from the heat. Keep an eye on the colour, also - if it starts going golden, remove it from the heat!

You can double check for doneness by dipping a spoon into the mixture, and immediately in to a bowl of ice water. Allow it to chill for 20 seconds or so, then remove. If you're happy with the texture - thick, gelatinous, and pretty firm without being brittle - remove mixture from the heat.
If mixture isn't firm enough when you text it in ice water, simmer a bit longer, testing for doneness every 1-2 minutes or so.

Immediately upon removing from the heat - working quickly - add in flavour mixture and tint with food colouring as desired, before pouring into prepared pan.

Once mixture is in the pan, do your best to spread it out in a thin, even layer. (Spraying the top with nonstick spray, laying a sheet of parchment on top, and then using another baking pan to flatten it is what I like to do!)

Cool to room temperature and allow to sit for several hours - or overnight - until very firm. Use a sharp knife to cut into strips (for bars), or bite sized square pieces. Spread out on a piece of plastic wrap and allow to sit for an hour or so before dipping in prepared Dipping Chocolate.

Transfer bars to parchment paper as they're dipped, allow to fully set before transferring to an airtight container for storage.

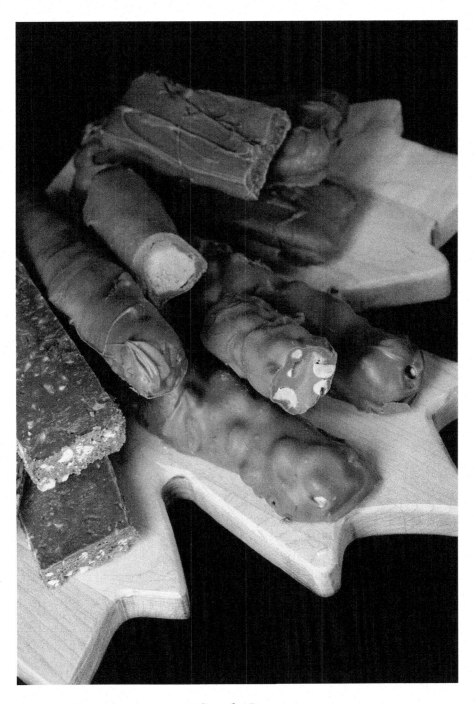

Candy Bars

"Passion Pastry" Squares

"Passion Pastry" Squares

These flaky little pastries are based on a convenience snack cake type pastry in Canada, but are definitely better homemade. Bonus: You can put more filling in them, than the source material!

Makes 18 pastries

Puff pastry, thawed	1 lb	500 g
Large egg, beaten	1	1
Cold water	1 Tbsp	15 ml
Granulated sugar, approximately:	1/4 cup	50 ml
Seedless raspberry jam, preserves, or jelly	½ cup	125 ml
Apple jelly	½ cup	125 ml
Marshmallow Creme Filling, Page 72		

Preheat oven to 400 F (200 C). Line 2 baking sheets with parchment paper.

Cut each of the 2 sheets of puff pastry into 9 squares, arrange on a prepared baking sheets.

Whisk egg and water together, brush over tops of squares, sprinkle generously with sugar.

Bake pastry for about 12 minutes, or until puffy and golden. Remove from oven, allow to cool to room temperature.

While waiting, mix together raspberry jam and apple jelly until well combined, set aside.

Using a serrated knife, carefully slice open each pastry square, forming two squares.

Spread the inside of one half with marshmallow cream filling, and the other with jelly mix. Sandwich 1 marshmallow side with 1 jelly side, repeat for all remaining pastry squares.

Individually wrap pastries, or place in an airtight container. Enjoy within a few hours, or store in the fridge for up to a week.

For Gluten-free: Use your favourite gluten-free puff pastry recipe, or store bought if you can find some!

Marshmallow Creme Filling

This filling is used for Passion Pastry Squares (Page 71) and "Joe Lewis" Cakes (page 74). One batch of filling is enough to do a batch each of those recipes!

Granulated sugar	3/4 cup	175 ml
Light corn syrup	½ cup	125 ml
Water	1/4 cup	50 ml
Large egg whites, at room temperature	2	2
Cream of tartar	1/4 tsp	1 ml
Salt	pinch	pinch
Milk	1 Tbsp	15 ml
Vanilla extract	2 tsp	10 ml
Icing (powdered/confectioner) sugar	1-2 cups	250-500 ml

In a small saucepan, whisk together sugar, corn syrup, and water. Affix a candy thermometer - making sure the tip is in the mixture, but NOT touching the bottom. Bring to a boil over high hear, whisking occasionally, until it reaches 240 F (115 C).

Right after putting your sugar mixture on the heat, have your egg whites whipping in a stand mixer: Using a whisk attachment, beat egg whites, cream of tartar, and salt together until soft peaks form. If it reaches soft peaks stage before the egg whites are ready, turn the mixer off and let it sit.

Once sugar mixture reaches 240 F (115 C), set mixer speed to low and slowly drizzle a small amount of hot sugar mixture into the egg whites. Continue *slowly* steaming small amounts of sugar syrup into the egg whites, until all of the syrup is fully incorporated.

Turn speed up to high, and whip for 5-7 minutes, until stiff and shiny. Turn mixer off. Add milk and vanilla, mix on low until incorporated. Add 1 cup of powdered sugar - slowly! - until well incorporated. Test for texture, add a little more powdered sugar if desired (for a stiffer filling), then beat on high for another minute.

Use right away, or store in an airtight container in the fridge until use. Will keep for about 2 weeks, though you may want to allow it to warm up slightly & re-whip it before use, if it firms up too much.

Creme Filling - for "June East" Cakes, page 76.

Heavy whipping cream	1 cup	250 ml
Vanilla extract	2 tsp	10 ml
Icing (powdered/confectioner) sugar	2 ½ cups	625 ml

Whip cream until soft peaks form. Add vanilla and powdered sugar - a little at a time - whipping until thick. Chill.

Buttercream - for "Yes, Caramel!" cakes, page 78.

Unsalted butter, softened	3 Tbsp	45 ml
Milk	1 Tbsp	15 ml
Salt	pinch	pinch
Icing (powdered/confectioner) sugar	2 cups	500 ml

Whip butter, milk, and salt until smooth and well combined. Add powdered sugar - a little at a time - whipping until very thick and smooth. If buttercream is too thick to pipe, add a small amount of milk and whip again until well incorporated. Carefully spoon mixture into pastry bags.

Marshmallow for Piping

This recipe is used for "Ox Cart Wheels" (Page 80), and "Long Live!" cookies (Page 82)

Unflavoured gelatin powder	2 ½ tsp	12 ml
Water, divided	½ cup	125 ml
Sugar	1 cup	250 ml
Corn Syrup	3 Tbsp	15 ml
Salt	pinch	pinch
Vanilla extract	1 tsp	5 ml

In a small bowl, sprinkle gelatin over about 1/4 cup water. Set aside.

In medium saucepan, combine sugar, corn syrup, remaining water, and salt. Cook over medium heat, stirring constantly, until sugar is dissolved. Bring to a boil and continue to cook - without stirring - until mixture reaches 240 F (115 C) on a candy thermometer. Remove from heat, add gelatin mixture, stirring until dissolved and completely combined.

Beat sugar syrup in a standing mixer - or with a hand held electric mixer - until it becomes thick, stiff, white, and almost triple the original volume. This may take up to 10 minutes. Once mixture is ready, add vanilla and beat until well incorporated. Carefully spoon mixture into pastry bags, use immediately.

"Joe Lewis" Cakes

This takes about half a batch of marshmallow creme filling, as does Passion Pastry Squares (Page 71) .. So I like to make a batch of each on the same day. Alternately, feel free to double this recipe. Pudding powder is optional, but yields a more moist cake.

Makes about 15 snack cakes

Cake flour	1 ½ cups	375 ml
Cocoa	1/4 cup	50 ml
Sugar	1 cup	250 ml
Instant vanilla pudding powder, optional	2 Tbsp	30 ml
Baking powder	1 Tbsp	15 ml
Salt	3/4 tsp	3 ml
Large eggs	3	3
Buttermilk*	3/4 cup	175 ml
Butter, melted	½ cup	125 ml
Vanilla extract	1 Tbsp	15 ml
Red food colouring		
Marshmallow Creme Filling, page 72		
Dipping Chocolate, page 67		

Preheat oven to 350 F (180 C). Liberally grease a 10" x 15" jelly roll pan. Line with parchment paper, then grease the parchment paper as well.

Combine flour, cocoa, sugar, pudding powder (if using), baking powder, and salt in a large mixing bowl. Add in eggs and buttermilk, beating until smooth. Carefully add melted butter and vanilla to the mix, mixing on medium speed until smooth. Use red food colouring to colour your batter - as vibrant or subtle as you want. Pour batter into prepared cake pan. Bake until cake pulls away from sides of pan, and center appears to be done - about 15 minutes. Remove from oven. Allow to cool 10-15 minutes.

Use a 3" cookie cutter to cut rounds from the cake - you should be able to get about 15. Set aside to fully cool, then use a sharp knife to split each in half, creating 2 thin circles. With the top and pan sides of the cake being the outsides, sandwich pairs of cake rounds together, with marshmallow creme filling on the inside. Set on a plate or baking sheet, wrap with plastic film, and chill for several hours. Once well chilled, carefully dip in warm Dipping Chocolate. Transfer to parchment paper and allow to fully set, before serving.

If you do not have buttermilk, stir 2 ½ tsp lemon juice or vinegar into 3/4 cup milk, and let sit for 5 minutes.

For Gluten-Free: Mix together 3/4 cup light buckwheat flour, 1/4 cup sorghum flour, 1/4 cup coconut flour, and ½ tsp xanthan gum. Use in place of cake flour

"Joe Lewis" Cakes

"June East" Cakes

Much like in "Joe Lewis" Cakes, the instant vanilla pudding powder is optional, but makes for a nicer, more moist cake when used.

Makes about 15 snack cakes

Cake flour	2 cups	500 ml
Sugar	1 cup	250 ml
Instant vanilla pudding powder, optional	2 Tbsp	30 ml
Baking powder	1 Tbsp	15 ml
Salt	3/4 tsp	3 ml
Large eggs	3	3
water	3/4 cup	175 ml
Butter, melted	½ cup	125 ml
Vanilla extract	1 Tbsp	15 ml
Creme Filling, page 73		
Dipping Chocolate, page 67		

Preheat oven to 350 F (180 C). Liberally grease a 10" x 15" jelly roll pan. Line with parchment paper, then grease the parchment paper as well.

Combine flour, sugar, baking powder, and salt in a large mixing bowl. Add in eggs and water, beating until smooth. Carefully add melted butter and vanilla to the mix, mixing on medium speed until smooth.

Pour batter into prepared cake pan. Bake until cake pulls away from sides of pan, and center appears to be done - about 15 minutes. Remove from oven. Allow to cool 10-15 minutes.

Use a 3" cookie cutter to cut rounds from the cake - you should be able to get about 15. Set aside to fully cool, then split each in half to create 2 thin circles.

With the top and pan sides of the cake being the outsides, sandwich pairs of cake rounds together, with Creme Filling on the inside. Set on a plate or baking sheet, wrap with plastic film, and chill for several hours.

Once well chilled, carefully dip in warm Dipping Chocolate. Transfer to parchment paper and allow to fully set, before serving.

For Gluten-Free: Mix together 1 1/4 cup light buckwheat flour, 1/4 cup sorghum flour, 1/4 cup coconut flour, and 3/4 tsp xanthan gum. Use in place of all-purpose flour.

"June East" Cakes

"Yes, Caramel!" Cakes

This "recipe" is more an assembly of other recipe parts, but I suppose that's to be expected when recreating different snack cakes from the same manufacturers - cakes, fillings, etc get mixed-and-matched across multiple products!

Of the cake based snack cakes covered here, these were my favourite. Much smaller - though they came 2 to a pack - and had a higher stuff-to-cake ratio, with the frosting and caramel on top. That may be why it was the second most requested snack cake recipe for this book, behind "Joe Lewis" Cakes.

Expats love their snack cakes, and there is usually no shortage of boxes of these - or "Joe Lewis" Cakes - in any "Look what I brought back with me!" Haul photos in expat groups!

Due to the very small amount of caramel needed for this recipe, I like to use store bought caramel ice cream topping. It's just not really worth the difficulty making such a small amount, as it can be more difficult to hit exactly the right temperature. For authenticity, buy the thickest variety you can find!

Makes about 35 snack cakes

"June East" Cake recipe, page 76
Buttercream, page 73
Thick caramel ice cream topping
Dipping Chocolate, page 67

Prepare and bake vanilla cake, per the directions in the "June East" Cakes recipe. Once cool, use a serrated knife to trim off any "hump" that may have occurred during baking.

Use a sharp knife or a cookie cutter to cut cake sheet into 2.5" squares.

Affix coupler and ½" diameter frosting tip to pastry bag, or just cut enough of the dip off to allow for a ½" diameter opening. Fill with fresh Buttercream, and pipe a circle on top of each cake square. Aim to keep all of the frosting on top of the cake, but close to or touching all 4 sides. You're building a "wall" to keep the caramel in. Chill cake for 20 minutes.

Carefully spoon caramel topping into the center of each frosting circle, filling them without overflowing them. Place cakes on baking sheet, freeze until caramel is firm.

Once frozen, carefully dip in warm Dipping Chocolate. Transfer to parchment paper and allow to fully set, before serving.

"Yes, Caramel!" Cakes

"Ox Cart Wheels"

These are typically sold alongside the snack cakes, but are more of a ... cookie? No cake involved, just two biscuits separated by a layer of marshmallow, the whole thing is dipped in chocolate. Growing up, we had these in our lunch boxes all the time! They're much easier to make than you may think - don't be intimidated by the marshmallow!

Makes about 15 sandwiches

Butter, softened	1/3 cup	75 ml
Brown sugar, packed	1/4 cup	50 ml
Granulated sugar	1/4 cup	50 ml
Large egg	1	1
Vanilla extract	½ tsp	2 ml
Baking powder	½ tsp	2 ml
Salt	1/4 tsp	1 ml
All purpose flour	1 1/4 cups	300 ml
Marshmallow for Piping, page 73		
Dipping Chocolate, page 67		

In a stand mixer, cream together butter and sugars until smooth and fluffy. Add in egg and vanilla extract, and mix until well incorporated and smooth. Mix remaining 3 ingredients together, carefully mix into wet ingredients until fully incorporated. Wrap dough in plastic film, chill for 1 hour.

Preheat oven to 350 F (180 C), line baking sheets with parchment paper.

On a floured counter, roll cookie dough out as thin as possible - 1/8" thick, ideally - and cut into 2.5-2.75" rounds. Place 2" apart on parchment lined baking sheet. Keeping a close eye on the cookies to avoid burning, bake cookies for 10-12 minutes, or until bottoms and edges look lightly golden. Allow cookies to cool on baking sheets for at least 5 minutes before moving. Cookies need to cool completely before proceeding.

As cookies are cooling, prepare Marshmallow for Piping recipe. Cut enough of the dip off the pastry bag to allow for a ½" diameter opening, pipe about ½" layer of marshmallow onto half of the cookies, evenly covering the entire top of each. Immediately top each with one of the remaining, non-marshmallowed cookies. Press gently to seal together, and allow cookies to sit, undisturbed, until fully set.

Once marshmallow has set, carefully dip sandwiches in warm Dipping Chocolate. Transfer to parchment paper and allow to fully set, before serving.

For Gluten-free: Mix together ½ cup brown rice flour, ½ cup sorghum flour, 2 Tbsp coconut flour, 1 Tbsp tapioca starch, 1 tsp xanthan gum. Use in place of all-purpose flour.

"Ox Cart Wheels"

"Long Live!" Cookies

These are probably my favourite cookie ever, and have been since I was young. I loved to carefully remove the cookie base from the marshmallow - as neatly as possible - and eat that (the lesser part!), before treating myself to the marshmallow, filling, and chocolate part.

As a child, they came in either raspberry or strawberry - I can't remember if it was one of those, or if both were available at the time - but now they're available in both of those flavours, as well as fudge - a chocolate filled one. So, if you'd like to be really authentic, use a strawberry or raspberry jam or preserves for this... just make sure it's seedless. If you want to go a little less authentic, but level it up a bit... go for blackcurrant. Not in the slightest bit authentic, but it's my favourite way to make these!

Note: In the source material, the top of the cookie is flat. When making these at home, getting that flat of a top while working with piped marshmallow would be a mess and frustrating, so I do them this way.

Makes about 50 cookies

Cookie recipe from "Ox Cart Wheels", page 80
Seedless jam of choice
Marshmallow for Piping, page 73
Dipping Chocolate, page 67

Prepare and bake cookie recipe, but with two small changes: Cut the cookies into 2" rounds, and bake for 8-10 minutes. Allow cookies to cool on baking sheets for at least 5 minutes before moving. Cookies need to cool completely before proceeding. As cookies are cooling, prepare Marshmallow for Piping recipe. Cut enough of the dip off the pastry bag to allow for a 1/4" diameter opening.

Use a small spoon - or a pastry bag - to put a small dollop of jam in the middle of each cookie, leaving a ½" border of un-jammed cookie around the edge. For each cookie, pipe a thick border of marshmallow that comes close to the edge of the cookie, ideally also touching the jam filling. Pipe a spiral around and over the jam - think "beehive" shaped. Completely enclose the jam, swirling at the top. Let go of pressure on the bag, and trail the remaining thread of marshmallow in a tight swirl to end it over top of the cookie, rather than drag it on to the next. (Mess!)

(You know, knowing a few apiarists, it is weird to type "beehive shaped" - meaning the sort of conical thing - where the only images I end up seeing of beehives are boxes. I wonder if most people picture boxes, or the mound shape? Hmm).

Repeat for remaining cookies, allow to rest for several hours, or until set. Once marshmallow has set, carefully dip sandwiches in warm Dipping Chocolate. Transfer to parchment paper and allow to fully set, before serving.

"Long Live!" Cookies

Lobster Roll

Main Dishes

Lobster Rolls

Lobster Rolls are an east coast delicacy, usually centered in Nova Scotia specifically. They're so popular, that you can buy them at some grocery stores, and even McDonald's sells a "McLobster" at times!

I consider Lobster Rolls to be almost a non-recipe, as there are a million ways of making it, all very dependant on personal taste. When it comes to an ingredient that is as expensive as lobster tends to be, you want to aim for your own tastes!

Start with your lobster. I like about 5 oz per roll, but 4oz / 1/4 lb is pretty typical of restaurants. Fresh is best, of course, but if you live inland, you may need to make some compromises there. Frozen tail meat can make a delicious sandwich, but I would stay away from pre-cooked frozen claw meat - I've never had a good experience with it. Next comes your bun. I like a soft but chewy bun. One of the local groceries in Minneapolis sells a "Bolillo roll" (it's not actually one) that is like a high end brat bun - LOVE it for this. Some people prefer a crispier roll, almost like a baguette. (And you could definitely use a section of baguette). I like mine cut and served as-is, though it's traditional to butter and grill / toast your bun. I don't like the mouth feel of that, so I skip it. I prefer the crunch to come from the celery!

Then there's the matter of mayo. Use the best quality mayo you can find, and only use enough of it to lightly coat your lobster. I think this is the only real "universal" tenet of lobster roll ingredients - do NOT use too much mayo! You want the lobster to shine, not be drowned in mayo. Once you have those basics together, think about the vegetables and flavourings you want. Onions or no? If yes, normal onions or green? Celery, or not? For me, my standard "while I live inland" Lobster Roll is (per roll):

Lobster tail meat	5 oz	140 g
Mayonnaise	1 ½ Tbsp	22 ml
Celery, sliced	½ rib	½ rib
White part of green onion, thinly sliced	1	1
Cracked mustard seed - just a sprinkle		
Fresh lemon zest - just a pinch		
Fresh dill - as much as I'm in the mood for		
Salt and pepper, to taste		

Boil or steam the lobster for no more than 10 minutes - overcooked lobster is tough lobster. Pick out all of the meat, allow to cool slightly, toss with remaining ingredients. Stuff into a roll, gluten-free if needed. Serve with kettle chips and a pickle spear.

Fish Cakes

Fish Cakes

Fish cakes are one of those foods that are pretty ubiquitous in coastal areas of Canada, though their composition can vary wildly. On the east coast, salt cod is commonly used, in a mashed potato base. Salt cod can be difficult to come by in many areas, though, so I tend to use fresh cod. You can make fish cakes that are closer to the mass produced, frozen kind - coated in bread crumbs - or you can make them more like a crab cake - fancy, clean, and more upscale feeling.

This recipe is my favourite version. It goes for the texture/shape of the traditional, mass produced ones (comfort food!), but incorporates flavours that would be more in line with a more upscale fish cake. I use corn flake crumbs to keep it gluten-free, but feel free to use panko bread crumbs, if you prefer. For this recipe, you can use cod or any other firm white fish - like haddock. If you're feeling adventurous, salmon or fresh tuna can also be used. When using salmon, I definitely like to use fresh dill in the mix, though I leave it out when using tuna.

Makes 4 servings

Large russet potatoes, peeled	3	3
Olive or vegetable oil		
Boneless fresh fish	1 lb	500 g
Salt and pepper		
Green onions, thinly sliced	1-2	1-2
Dijon mustard	2 tsp	10 ml
Fresh dill, chopped (optional)	1 Tbsp	15 ml
Large egg, beaten	1	1
Corn flake crumbs (Approx. measurement)	1 cup	250 ml

Peel and chop potatoes into large chunks of roughly equal size. Place chopped potatoes into a medium sized pot, cover with hot water, and boil for about 20 minutes, or until tender. Strain, transfer to a large bowl, mash, and set aside.

Heat about 2 Tbsp oil in a frying pan. Place fish in pan, sprinkle with a little salt and pepper, and cook - flipping to cook on both sides - until opaque and flakes easily when prodded with a fork. Remove from heat. Add fish to bowl of mashed potatoes, use a fork to flake/mash the fish into small pieces. Add green onions, mustard, and dill, if using. Taste, season with salt, pepper, and more dill if desired. Add egg, mix until well distributed. Cover bowl, chill for 10 minutes.

Divide fish mixture into 8 evenly sized balls. Form into patties, roll in corn flake or bread crumbs, pressing to secure. Transfer each cake to a plate or baking sheet lined with parchment paper. Wipe fry pan out, add another 2 Tbsp oil. Heat oil over medium heat, add a few fish cakes - don't crowd the pan - and pan fry until golden brown, crispy, and heated through. Repeat with remaining fish cakes. Serve hot, with tartar sauce, lemon wedges, and/or more fresh dill.

Cod Au Gratin

Cod Au Gratin

Cod au gratin isn't something I was raised on, but a dish I was exposed to while living in Newfoundland - it's VERY popular there, with many people and restaurants all having their own take on it. It's a highly customizable dish! Cheddar is traditional, but you can use white cheddar, havarti, provolone, or any other mild cheese. Beer - gluten-free beer, if necessary - can be substituted for the wine (this is especially good with cheddar). You can leave the savoury out, or substitute parsley, chives, or any other herb you enjoy with mild fish. Sometimes, I'll add chopped up asparagus or broccoli, just to convince myself that it's healthy!

Makes 4-6 servings

Boneless cod loins, thawed and drained	2 lbs	1 kg
Butter	1/4 cup	50 ml
Small onion, finely chopped	½	½
Garlic cloves, pressed or minced	1-2	1-2
All-purpose flour	2 Tbsp	30 ml
Prepared Dijon mustard	1 Tbsp	15 ml
Dry white wine	1/4 cup	50 ml
Milk	2 1/4 cups	550 ml
Shredded Parmesan cheese	2/3 cup	150 ml
Shredded cheddar cheese	1 cup	250 ml
Dried summer savoury	2 tsp	10 ml
Salt & pepper		
Plain potato chips, crumbled	Small bag	Small bag

Preheat oven to 350 F (180 C). Cut cod into 1" pieces, arrange in an 8x8" baking pan. Alternately, you can divide them between 4-6 individual ramekins. Set aside.

In a medium sauce pan, melt butter. Add onion and garlic and cook - stirring frequently - until onions are tender and translucent. Add flour to the pot, cook for another minute, stirring frequently. Add Dijon, whisking until well incorporated. Carefully add wine to pot, whisking until smooth. Cook for 2 minutes, whisking frequently. Add milk, once again whisking until smooth. Heat until mixture starts to thicken. Once sauce mixture starts to thicken, add half of the Parmesan and a small handful of the cheddar, stirring until thick, melted, and smooth. Add savoury, season with salt and pepper, to taste.

Pour sauce over fish, stirring to coat and distribute evenly. Scatter cheddar cheese across the top of the fish mixture, then remaining Parmesan. Spread crumbled potato chips on top. Bake – uncovered- for about 35 (individual ramekins) - 50 minutes (8x8 pan), or until fish is cooked through, and sauce is bubbly. Serve hot.

For gluten-free: Omit all purpose flour, use 1/4 cup potato starch in its place.

Seafood Chowder

Seafood Chowder

When I was living in Newfoundland, I ate the best chowder - literally anywhere I would go! Unlike the delicate clam chowders I'd had before that time, these were loaded with multiple types of fish and shellfish, big chunks of goodness - very hearty. It pretty much wrecked me for clam chowder. So, this isn't the cheapest dish to make, especially for those of us who live inland. It makes a fair amount.. and it's fairly quick & easy to make.

Makes 6-8 servings

Boneless cod loins	2 lbs	1 kg
Boneless salmon fillet	1 lb	500 g
Medium or large shrimp	1 lb	500 g
Bay scallops	½ lb	250 g
Butter	1/4 cup	50 ml
Large onion	1	1
Ribs celery, chopped or sliced	3	3
Large carrot, peeled and sliced	1	1
Large parsnip, peeled and sliced	1	1
Large yellow or red potatoes	4	4
Garlic cloves, pressed or minced	4	4
Seafood, chicken or vegetable stock	8 cups	2 L
Butter	½ cup	125 ml
All-purpose flour	½ cup	125 ml
White wine (Or more stock)	1 cup	250 ml
Heavy cream	3 cups	750 ml

Dried summer savoury (optional), salt and pepper

Chop cod loins and salmon into bite sized pieces. Add to a large bowl along with shrimp and bay scallops, chill until ready to use.

In a large pot, melt butter. Add onion, celery, carrots, and parsnips to the pot, sauté just until onion and celery soften and go translucent - don't brown them. Chop potatoes into bite sized pieces, add to the pot along with garlic and stock. Bring to a boil, reduce heat slightly and simmer for 10 minutes.

While soup is boiling, make a light roux: In a medium saucepan, melt remaining butter. Add flour, whisk until smooth. Cook, stirring constantly, for 1 minute. Add white wine, whisking until smooth. Add heavy cream, once again whisking until smooth. Allow mixture to heat just to steaming. Add seafood and cream mixture to the main pot, gently stir well to combine. Allow to cook for 5 to 10 minutes - without coming to a boil - or until the seafood is cooked through and chowder has thickened. Season with savoury, salt and pepper to taste, serve hot.

For gluten-free: Omit all purpose flour, use 2/3 cup white rice flour in its place.

French Canadian Pea Soup

French Canadian Pea Soup

Ah, pea soup. I love French Canadian style – loved it when I was a kid – especially when served at Festival du Voyageur activities in my hometown!

I loved it when I first moved out on my own, living on the cheap, and was buying the "Habitant" canned stuff like it was going out of style.

Now, as an expatriate Canadian... I may love it even more! Unlike many of the other homeland foods I adore, this one is easily made, with almost all of the ingredients being available locally. Sure, you can't get *proper* summer savoury in Minnesota – but you CAN beg friends to bring some back from vacations on Canada's east coast! (Thank you Amanda, Laura and Andrew... you're awesome and I adore you for it!)

This makes a LOT of soup. Because soup isn't an everyday kind of thing to make, I like to make a large batch, and freeze most of it – it freezes / thaws beautifully.

This version is a bit easier than the 100% traditional way, which uses a ham bone in it. Feel free to add a ham bone in with the water, pulling it out as the mixture gets thick, though. I just find it convenient to use the small, boneless ham chunks for this.

Be sure to have plenty of crusty baguette on hand for serving this.

Olive Oil	1 Tbsp	15 ml
Large onions, chopped	3	3
Grated celery	2 cups	500 ml
Dried yellow split peas	3 lbs	1500 g
Water	24 cups	5.5 L
Cured ham, cut into bite sized pieces	3 lbs+	1500 g+
Grated carrots (about 6 carrots)	1 cup	250 ml
Dried summer savoury	1 Tbsp	15 ml
Bay leaf	1	1
Ground black pepper	2 tsp	10 ml
Salt		

In a LARGE pot, saute onions and celery in olive oil, cooking until tender and translucent. Add split peas, water, ham, and carrots, bring to a boil. Cover pot, remove from heat, and allow to sit for one hour.

After one hour, return pot to heat and bring up to a boil once more. Add summer savoury, bay leaf, and pepper. Simmer over medium heat until split peas break down, forming a very thick soup.

Remove bay leaf, season with salt to taste, serve hot.

Chicken Fricot

Chicken Fricot

This is a simple Acadian dish with clean flavours, especially popular in areas of Nova Scotia and New Brunswick. Like many regional specialties, it can be made in a multitude of ways, with a variety of ingredient or technique differences. While fricot can be made with various meats or fish, chicken is most popular. As far as technique goes, I've gone with a less labour intensive version than some which can involve a whole chicken. The savoury really makes the dish, and sometimes I'll add 2 cloves of garlic .. though this isn't traditional at all.

Makes about 8 servings

Butter	2 Tbsp	30 ml
Large onion, chopped	1	1
Boneless skinless chicken thighs, chopped	3 lbs	1500 g
Carrots, sliced	3	3
Celery ribs, sliced	2	2
All purpose flour	1 Tbsp	15 ml
Chicken broth	8 cups	2 L
Red or gold potatoes, peeled & chopped	2 lbs	1 kg
Dried summer savoury	2 tsp	10 ml
All-purpose flour	2 cups	500 ml
Dried summer savoury	2 tsp	10 ml
Baking powder	4 tsp	20 ml
Salt	1 tsp	5 ml
Milk	1 cup	250 ml
Salt and pepper		

In a large, heavy pot, cook onion in butter until just it starts to go translucent. Add chicken thighs, cook until outside browns slightly. Add carrots and celery, cook for one minute. Sprinkle flour over chicken and vegetables, toss to coat, cook for one more minute. Add broth, potatoes, and savoury. Stir well, bring to a boil, and set a timer for 35 minutes.

In a medium sized bowl, mix together flour, savoury, baking powder, and salt. Add milk , stir just until dough comes together. Don't over stir or beat it. If dough is too crumbly, add a small amount of extra milk. If the dough is sticky, add a small amount of flour. Divide into 8 loose balls. Once timer goes off, season Fricot with salt and pepper, to taste. Drop dumplings into the soup, spacing out evenly. Cover and simmer for 15 minutes WITHOUT LIFTING THE LID. Serve hot.

For Gluten-free: Omit all all-purpose flour in the recipe. Use 1 Tbsp light buckwheat flour in the soup, and a mix of 1 cup light buckwheat flour, 2/3 cup millet flour, 1/3 cup potato flour, and 2 tsp tapioca starch in the dumplings. Increase milk to 2/3 cup.

Chicken Souvlaki

Souvlaki

When asking for what recipes fellow Canadian expats wanted in this book, souvlaki came up frequently. Yes, it's a Greek dish... but for some reason, a lot of Canadians living away can't find GOOD souvlaki - if they can find it at all! Yes, we get spoiled for various ethnic foods in Canada!

I like to start this out the night before: Marinating the chicken, and allowing the yogurt to strain in the fridge. The next morning, I finish making the tzatziki, and return it to the fridge. Chilling the finished tzatziki for a few hours allows the flavours to come together nicely. While this is written as a chicken recipe, feel free to use pork tenderloin, or even lamb. To serve as shown, slice up 1 tomato, 1 cucumber, and 1 red onion. Serve souvlaki on warmed pitas, with plenty of tzatziki. Serves 4

Boneless skinless chicken	2 lbs	1 kg
Olive oil	1/4 cup	50 ml
Lemon juice	1/4 cup	50 ml
Lemon, zest of	1	1
Garlic cloves, minced or pressed	4	4
Dried oregano	1 Tbsp	15 ml
Salt	½ tsp	2 ml
Ground black pepper	½ tsp	2 ml
Plain yogurt	3 cups	750 ml
English cucumber, peeled	1	1
Salt	½ tsp	2 ml
Garlic cloves, pressed	3	3
Lemon juice	1 Tbsp	15 ml
Chopped fresh dill	1 Tbsp	15 ml
Salt and pepper, to taste		

Trim chicken breasts, cut into 1" cubes. Place prepared chicken into a non-metallic bowl or dish (with a lid). In a large bowl, whisk together olive oil, lemon juice, lemon zest, garlic, oregano, salt, and pepper. Pour marinade over chicken, stir well to coat. Chill for at least 2 hours, or overnight.

Line a metal strainer with 2 layers of cheesecloth, place over a smaller bowl. Place yogurt into cheesecloth, chill in the fridge overnight.

Grate the peeled cucumber, squeeze out as much water as you can. Place grated cucumber into a bowl, stir in ½ tsp salt, allow to sit for 10 minutes. Squeeze out remaining water. Mix together strained yogurt, squeezed cucumber, garlic, lemon juice, and dill; season with salt and pepper to taste. Cover and chill for at least 1 hour before serving.

Thread chicken onto skewers, grill until chicken is cooked through. Serve hot, with tzaziki sauce, vegetables, and pita.

Donairs

Donairs

This east coast specialty is something like a gyro, but all beef - no lamb. Rather than the traditional tzatziki sauce, donairs use "donair sauce". For gluten-free, use gluten-free pitas.

Medium onion	1	1
Lean ground beef	3 lbs	1 ½ kg
Corn starch	1 Tbsp	15 ml
Garlic powder	1 Tbsp	15 ml
Ground black pepper	2 tsp	10 ml
Oregano	2 tsp	10 ml
Cayenne powder	1 ½ tsp	7 ml
Salt	1 ½ tsp	7 ml
Paprika	1 tsp	5 ml
Sweetened condensed milk (1 can)	14 oz	396 g
White vinegar	1/3 cup	75 ml
Garlic powder	1 tsp	5 ml
Pitas	6-8	6-8
Onion, thinly sliced	1	1
Tomato, chopped	1	1

Preheat oven to 325 F (160 C). Peel and chop onion, pulse in a food processor until pureed. Dump onion puree into the middle of 2-3 layers of paper towels or cheesecloth; gather the edges and squeeze all of the liquid from the onions. Return onion solids to the food processor, discard liquid.

Add about 1 lb of the ground beef, the corn starch, spices and salt to the food processor, process until it's a creamy paste. Add another lb of beef, process again until smooth. Add remaining beef, process once again until smooth, scraping down the sides of the food processor to ensure that everything is smooth. Form meat mixture into a large log shape, place onto a broiling pan/rack. Bake for 2 hours, flipping loaf over at the halfway point. Once 2 hours are up, remove from oven, allow to cool to room temperature. Wrap cooled loaf in plastic wrap, chill for at least 8 hours, or overnight.

In a medium mixing bowl, combine sweetened condensed milk, vinegar, and garlic powder. Use a whisk to mix together the sauce ingredients - it'll take some time, but it will eventually come together. Once well combined and thick, transfer to a covered container, chill until use.

To Assemble: Brush pitas with a little water, heat in a hot frying pan until warmed through. Heat a little vegetable oil in a frying pan. Slice donair meat into 1/4" thick slices, add to pan and reheat until desired texture (If you like the crispy edges, cook a little longer than you would if you don't!). Pile reheated meat on warm pita, drizzle generously with sauce, top with onions and tomatoes. Wrap in wax paper, parchment paper, or foil to hold it together while eating, serve immediately.

Fish N Chips

Fish N Chips

Having spent some time on the east coast, I KNOW good fish and chips. Crispy, golden batter, encasing tender, juicy fish. Douse it in proper vinegar... oh yeah. This recipe will NOT disappoint even those who are Fish N Chips purists.

Now, vinegar can be a bit of a sticking point for some gluten-free people. Much like with whiskey, most experts/associations agree that all vinegar is gluten free - even malt vinegar, which is distilled from a wheat preparation. However, some people find themselves reacting to malt vinegar - so exercise caution if you require gluten-free.

Serves 4

Oil for frying		
All-purpose flour	1 cup	250 ml
Baking powder	1 Tbsp	15 ml
Salt	1 tsp	5 ml
Ground black pepper	½ tsp	2 ml
Onion powder	1/4 tsp	1 ml
Garlic powder	1/4 tsp	1 ml
Large egg, beaten	1	1
Cold beer	1 ½ cups	375 ml
Fresh Cod loins or fillets	2 lbs	1 kg
Salt and pepper		
All-purpose flour, for dredging	1 cup	250 ml
Fries, recipe on page 32		

Start heating your oil to 350 F (180 C) – you'll want at least 2-3" of oil in your pot or deep fryer.

In a large bowl, combine flour, baking powder, salt, pepper, and onion/garlic powders. Add egg and beer, stir well to form a thick batter. All batter to sit for 5 minutes or so.

Season fish fillets with salt and pepper. Gently dredge fish in flour, shaking excess back into the bowl. One piece at a time, dip into batter, allowing excess batter to drip back into bowl for a few seconds, before carefully transferring to heated oil.

Fry for a few minutes on each side, until golden brown and cooked through. Use a slotted metal spoon to transfer fried fish to paper towels. Allow oil to come back up to temperature between batches. Serve hot, with fries and vinegar.

For Gluten-free: Omit all purpose flour. Use 1 ½ cups garbonzo (chickpea) flour and ½ cup white rice flour in batter. Use gluten-free beer or cold water. Dredge fish with either more garbanzo flour, or corn starch.

Ginger Beef

Ginger Beef

While Ginger Beef is widely available in most areas of Canada, it's very much an iconic thing in Alberta, where beef is a major industry.

As with most iconic dishes, there's a degree of variety in how different restaurants prepare this. Some add snow peas, others do not. Some use red pepper, others do not. Some are sweeter than others, others are spicier than others. This is a good base recipe, but - depending on your memory of ginger beef - may be tweaked to suit you!

Additionally, feel free to play with the thickness of the beef. The thinner the slice of beef, the crispier the finished product. If you like it a bit chewier / meatier, cut it a bit thicker.

Serves 4

Flank steak	1 lb	500 g
Carrot	1	1
Small onion	1	1
Green bell pepper	1	1
Red bell pepper	1	1
Green onions	4	4
Celery stalk	1	1
Knob of fresh ginger	~3"	~ 7.5 cm
Garlic cloves, pressed or minced	5	5
Corn starch	1 cup	250 ml
All-purpose flour	½ cup	125 ml
Ground black pepper	1 tsp	5 ml
Large egg	1	1
Water	1 cup	250 ml

Oil for frying - I use vegetable oil

Olive or sesame oil	1 Tbsp	15 ml
Soy sauce - low sodium	1/3 cup	75 ml
Water or beef stock	1/3 cup	75 ml
Honey	1/4 cup	50 ml
Rice vinegar	2 Tbsp	30 ml
Cooking wine	1 Tbsp	15 ml
Crushed chilies / red pepper flakes	1 ½ tsp	7 ml

Trim beef if necessary, freeze for about 20 minutes to firm it up. Slice beef along the grain, into long, very thin strips, chill while preparing other ingredients.

Prepare veggies: Peel your carrot and onion, seed the peppers. Julienne the carrot and peppers, slice onion into long, thin slices. Slice green onions into thin strips, on a diagonal. "Star Trek" your celery (Thin slices on a diagonal, "communicator badge" shape!).

Peel the ginger, and prepare as you like: I like to finely mince it, some like it julienned. Add all vegetable and root pieces to a large bowl, along with garlic, set aside.

In a large bowl, combine cornstarch, flour and pepper. Add egg and water, stir well to form a thick batter. If gluten-free, allow batter to sit for 10 minutes or so, to soften the rice flour.

With all of your ingredients prepared, start heating your oil to 375F – you'll want at least 2-3" of oil in your pot or deep fryer. When oil is heated, toss marinated beef strips in batter, fry in small batches until golden and crispy. Use a slotted metal spoon to transfer fried beef to paper towels.

As beef is frying, stir fry veggies in olive or sesame oil until they start to soften a little. Add soy sauce, water/beef stock, honey, rice vinegar, cooking wine, and crushed chilies. Bring to a boil, reduce heat, and simmer on medium-low until beef is all fried.

Add fried beef to the pan, stir until well coated. Serve immediately for crispy beef, or allow to simmer on low for 20 minutes or so for a more authentic takeout texture/taste. Best served over rice.

For Gluten-free: Mix together 1/4 cup light buckwheat flour and 1/4 cup white rice flour, use in place of all-purpose flour. Be sure to use a gluten-free soy sauce

Tourtière

Proper Tourtière ("Tortière", for some) a wonderful thing. Tourtière is a French Canadian meat pie, and it's SO good when made properly.

There are probably as many ways to make it, as there are people in Quebec. Some people use mashed potatoes, some use cubed potatoes... some will skip the carrots, others may skip the celery. This is my way... and I'm 50% French-Canadian, so it's at least halfway "legit"!

Serves about 8

Ground pork	1 lb	500 g
Ground beef	1 lb	500 g
Small onion, finely chopped	1	1
Celery ribs , finely chopped	4	4
Carrots, grated	2	2
Fresh parsley, chopped	½ cup	125 ml
Large potatoes, peeled, cut into 1/3" cubes	2	2
Dried summer savoury	1-2 Tbsp	15-30 ml
Ground black pepper	2-3 tsp	10-15 ml
Bay leaves	2	2
Salt	1 tsp	5 ml
Ground cloves	1/4 tsp	1 ml
Milk	2 cups	500 ml
Beef or chicken broth	1 ½ cups	375 ml

2 pre-made pie crusts, or double pie crust recipe of choice, prepared.

Large egg	1	1
Cold water	1 Tbsp	15 ml

Combine meats, vegetables, and seasonings together in a large pan or pot, stirring until everything is relatively uniform. Add the milk and the broth, stirring once again. Bring mixture to a boil, then turn the heat down to medium and simmer – stirring often – until the liquid has cooked off, and the meat has broken down almost to a paste. This should take about an hour, give or take. Once it's ready, remove from heat and cool to room temperature.

Preheat oven to 425 F (220 C).

Line a deep dish pie pan with one pie crust, carefully working it into the corners. Fill pie pan with meat filling, spreading it into the corners and mounding it in the center.

Use the second pie crust to cover the pie filling. Crimp the edges as desired, poke a couple of slits in it. If desired, roll any extra dough very thin, cut into shapes, and apply to the crust for decoration. Whisk together egg and water, brush over the entire top of the pie.

Bake at 20 minutes, turn heat down to 375 F (190 C) and continue to bake for another 15 minutes, until crust is golden brown.

Serve warm or cold.

For Gluten-free: Use the following crust recipe for the one included in this recipe.

Gluten-Free Crust for Tourtière

Sorghum flour	3/4 cup	175 ml
Amaranth flour	½ cup	125 ml
Corn starch	½ cup	125 ml
Millet flour	½ cup	125 ml
Potato starch (plus more for rolling)	1/3 cup	75 ml
Tapioca starch	2 Tbsp	30 ml
Xanthan gum	2 tsp	10 ml
Butter, softened	½ cup	125 ml
Cream cheese, softened	8 oz	250 g
Large egg	1	1

Combine flours, starches, and xanthan gum, whisking well to combine. Set aside.

Beat butter and cream cheese until well mixed and soft. Slowly add dry ingredients, mixing until a dough comes together. Generously dust work surface with additional potato starch, turn dough out and knead until smooth. Form a disk, wrap tightly in plastic wrap, and refrigerate for about 30 minutes.

Divide dough into 2 parts, roll each out to 1/4" thick or so, use as directed in the recipe.

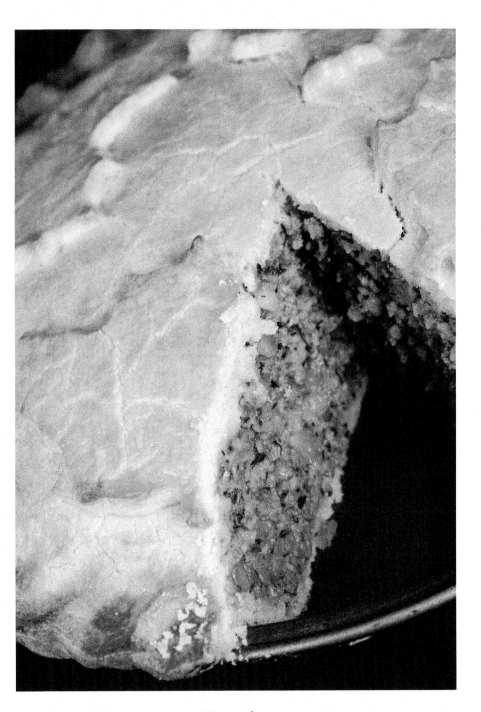

Tourtière

Rappie Pie

Rappie Pie

Rappie pie is an Acadian dish, popular in Nova Scotia and New Brunswick. It's made from "patates râpées" - grated/shredded potatoes, hence the name.

The liquid is removed from the potatoes, and replaced with broth. The râpée potato mixture encloses a meat mixture - usually chicken, but turkey, beef, pheasant, rabbit, seafood, etc can also be used. It's baked for a fairly long time, until golden and crispy. It can be served as-is, but is also popularly chilled overnight and fried in a pan, served up with butter and molasses.

The amount of broth added to the potato mixture can vary, depending on how much liquid you get out of the potatoes in the first place, and how you like your rappie pie - some areas lean more towards runnier, as a general rule.. .while others tend to go for thicker, more solid râpée. Personally, I like mine a bit thicker and solid, as it's easier to slice and fry.

The broth is the key to success in this recipe - you want it flavourful! This is the area with the most room for personal interpretation, so feel free to swap or add stock vegetables, change the seasoning up, etc. With this dish, it's important to keep the broth hot and work quickly, as the potatoes brown very fast when you take the water out.

Makes about 10 servings

Large chicken	1	1
Large onions	3	3
Celery ribs	4	4
Carrots, peeled	2	2
Salt and pepper		
Dried summer savoury (optional)		
Garlic cloves	2-3	2-3
Russet potatoes	10 lbs	4 ½ kg
Butter		
Bacon or pork fat	1/4 lb	125 g

Cut chicken into several large pieces, place into a large stock pot. Peel 2 of the onions, chop into large pieces. Place onions, celery, and carrots into pot. Add just enough water to cover the chicken. Bring to a boil, turn heat down to a simmer, and allow to simmer gently for 2-3 hours.

Once time is up - and you have a richly flavoured broth - strain the stock into a large bowl. Rinse pot, return strained stock to pot and place over low heat to keep warm. Taste, season with salt, pepper, and savoury.

Discard vegetables, allow chicken to cool enough to handle. Once cool, remove chicken meat from the bones, discard bones. Chop remaining onion, peel garlic and press. Add onion and garlic to chicken meat, set aside.

Preheat oven to 450 F (230 C), bring stock up to a boil.

Wash and peel potatoes. Grate by hand, by stand mixer attachment, or in a food processor.

In batches, place grated potatoes in the center of 2 pieces of cheese cloth, gather the edges, and squeeze out all of the juice. Save all of the juice being squeezed out - you'll want to measure it when you're done with the potatoes!

Measure the liquid removed from the potatoes - this is the amount of stock you'll be adding to the potatoes. Once you know the total amount, discard potato juice.

In a large bowl, add the measured chicken stock to the potatoes, a little at a time. The goal is to get the consistency somewhere between apple sauce, and mashed potatoes - you may need more or less than the amount you measured off the potatoes. Once mixture has reached the right consistency, taste and adjust seasonings if necessary.

Butter a large foil roaster pan. Pour ½ of the potato mixture into the pan, spreading evenly. Top with chicken, onion, and garlic mixture, sprinkling it evenly over potato base. Gently top with remaining potato mixture, again spreading evenly.

Chop pork fat or bacon, if using, and sprinkle randomly over the top of the rappie pie. Place in preheated oven, bake for 40 minutes. Turn heat down to 375 and bake for another 2 hours, until a golden crust has formed on top.

Serve hot!

Perogies

Growing up in Winnipeg, my grandmother used to make amazing perogies, and I've never forgotten that. Most other perogies - especially since moving away from Winnipeg - pales in comparison! Shortly after moving to the USA, I had to call her up for her recipe, which she supplied with an endless stream of tips.

I've developed this adaptation to be a little less intimidating of an undertaking. While I recall perogy making as being an all day thing, this should take about 2 hours from start to finish. The recipe is easily scalable, though, so if you'd like to make an all day thing of it, have at it! Theoretically, you can freeze these - individually on a baking sheet, then bag them together when frozen - but unless you make several batches (or don't really like perogies!), they'll never make it to the freezer!

Makes 4 or 5 dozen perogies

Large eggs	2	2
Salt	½ tsp	2 ml
Vegetable oil	½ cup	125 ml
Lukewarm water	2 cups	500 ml
All-purpose flour	5-6 cups	1250-1500 ml
Red potatoes	3 lbs	1 ½ kg
Cheese, shredded *	1 ½ -2 lbs	750g - 1kg
Bacon, optional*	1 lb	500 g
Sauerkraut, well drained, optional*	1 lb	500 g
Cottage cheese, optional*	1 lb	500 g
Finely chopped onion, optional*		
Dill Weed, optional*		
Butter, melted		

Beat eggs, add salt and oil, beat until mixed together well. Add water, beat again. Add 5 cups flour and mix well, adding more flour if sticky. Lightly knead until well incorporated and smooth. Cover bowl with plastic wrap and allow to rest for one hour. While waiting, work on filling.

Peel potatoes, cut into roughly equal sized pieces. Boil in a large pot of water until tender, drain well. I like to use my KitchenAid to mash my potatoes, and it works doubly well for this. You can, however, always mash and mix by hand. Either way, mash potatoes until smooth, and mix in your choice of cheese and flavourings until well incorporated. Cover and set aside

Roll out dough on floured counter top. Aim to get it pretty thin – 1/16 – 1/8" of an inch or so. When you're first starting out, a bit thicker is ok – you'll just have a bit more dough to bite through to get to your yummy filling!

Cut dough with large glass or round cookie cutter – I like to use a glass that's about 3" in diameter.

Place 1 tbsp of filling in the center of each round, lightly brush the edges with water, which will act as a glue.

Pick one round up in your non-dominant hand, and use your dominant hand to fold the dough around the filling, sealing the edge from one side to the other, squeezing most of the air out, as you go. Make sure your perogies are sealed well, or they will explode when you cook them! Also, I like to flatten them out a little.

Heat a large pot of water to a low boil - too rolling of a boil will rip your perogies apart! Drop a few perogies in at a time – our 1 gallon pot is good for about a dozen. Cook until all rise to the surface, then for 2-3 minutes longer. Remove cooked perogies from water, lightly toss with melted butter. This will prevent them from sticking together.

Enjoy as-is, or fry them in butter, onions.. maybe with some Kielbasa sausage… serve with some sour cream.. YUM!

* Filling Variations

Traditional: 2 lbs sharp Cheddar cheese.

Onion, Bacon, and Cheese: 1 ½ lbs cheddar cheese of your choice, 1 lb crisp bacon (crumbled), chopped onion to taste.

Sauerkraut: Add 1 lb (or more) sauerkraut to your potatoes. Cheese is optional – up to you!

Cottage Cheese, Onion, and Dill: 1 lb well drained cottage cheese (or more, whatever!), onion and dill weed to taste.

The beauty of perogies is that you can customize your fillings in SO many ways. Have fun with it!

Technique Variation:

Grandma was very adamant that perogy making is time consuming, and that – rather than cutting the dough into rounds, taking the scraps, and re-rolling/cutting more – I should DEFINITELY use her technique. I don't. Sorry, gramma! In case you'd like to, here it is:

Roll your dough out, and cut into 3" wide strips. Cut those again into 3" squares, place filling in the middle, and fold/seal them to make triangles. Yes, it would be quicker than the rounds – I just don't have the big hatred for cutting rounds that she did!

For Gluten Free: Ignore ingredients in main recipe, use these amounts instead. Makes a smaller batch, about 3 dozen perogies. (Feel free to double it!)

Sour cream	1 cup	250 ml
Large eggs	2	2
Warm milk	1/4 cup	50 ml
Vegetable oil	1/4 cup	50 ml
Tapioca starch	2/3 cup	150 ml
Sweet rice flour	1/3 cup	75 ml
Potato starch	1/3 cup	75 ml
Corn starch	1/3 cup	75 ml
Sorghum flour	1 cup	250 ml
Salt	½ tsp	2 ml
Xanthan gum	2 tsp	10 ml
Extra potato starch, for rolling		

In a food processor or stand mixer, blitz/beat sour cream, eggs, milk, and oil together until well combined. In a separate bowl, whisk together remaining ingredients (except extra potato starch) until well combined. Add to wet ingredients, blitz/beat until a sticky dough comes together. Wrap dough in plastic film, allow to rest on counter for 45 minutes. While waiting, work on the filling, using the instructions in the main recipe:

Red potatoes, peeled and quartered	1 ½ lbs	750 g
Cheddar cheese, shredded	½ - 3/4 lb	250-375 g
Optional flavourings*		

Jiggs Dinner

Jiggs Dinner

While I had had "special" roast dinners growing up - Christmas, Thanksgiving, etc - they were definitely a once-in-a-blue-moon, special occasion thing.

When I moved to Newfoundland, I learned of the whole Sunday Dinner ritual there - full roasts, stuffing, sides - Jiggs Dinner. It was "traditional" in that, well, it was tradition... but unlike most traditions, this one was immensely commonplace. Unlike many traditional roast dinners, etc, Salt Meat and Jiggs Dinner weren't specifically relegated to special occasions; Though you may go more all-out on a special occasion, Jiggs Dinner is served in restaurants year round, and monthly or even weekly in homes.

Man, this is really hard to write about. After 11 years in Minnesota, all I really want is to go sit at my "thinking spot" in Petty Harbour, just breathing in the clean air, smelling the ocean, the seaweed, and the fish (I know. I KNOW. I love that smell though!). I would find any excuse to go lay on a rock by the ocean, thinking about anything, everything... nothing. Didn't matter. That air... I can still smell it, in my head. Sigh.

Anyway, Sundays were a great excuse to make the drive, as I'd just tell myself that I had to buy my salt beef from Bidgood's, a grocer along the way. Never mind that there were many decent grocery stores between my place and there, of course.

Jiggs Dinner isn't so much a recipe, as it is a set of rough guidelines / order of operations, and - for the purposes of this book - a series of sub recipes. Add or subtract ingredients as necessary, season to your own taste. First off, decide your menu. A typical Jiggs Dinner will include some or all of the following:

- Some kind of roast (Turkey, chicken, or pork usually)
- Dressing
- Gravy
- Salt beef
- Pease pudding
- Potatoes
- carrots
- Parsnips
- Turnips
- Cabbage or turnip greens
- Mustard pickles
- Pickled beets
- A boiled pudding, usually blueberry duff or figgy duff. Optionally served with sauce.

Then, plan out your time lime / order of operations. Some of this will depend on the type of roast you're cooking (turkey takes much longer than a pork loin!), what all you're including, and your taste in terms of how soft the vegetables are.

As an example, this is how I do it:

The night before: Soak peas in water

Variable, depending on roast: Prepare dressing and roast, put in the oven

3 hours before mealtime: Salt beef and pease pudding go in a LARGE pot to boil

1.5 hours before: Put on the duff

40-45 minutes before: Cabbage gets chopped into wedges, goes in the pot

35-40 minutes before: Carrots, turnips, parsnips get peeled, cut into large chunks, go in the pot

25 minutes before: Potatoes get washed, cut into large chunks, go in the pot

10 minutes before: Start a roux for the gravy

5 minutes before: Take chicken out, use pan juices to finish gravy

Dinner time before: Strain everything, mash pease pudding, serve everything

When you make the sauce for the duff depends on whether you're using one or not (many forgo it altogether), and what you feel like doing. You can make it ahead and reheat, you can make it just before - or at the same time - as the gravy, or you can wait until after dinner, and make it just before serving it as a separate dessert.

Now, the recipes!

Sweet Mustard Pickles

In addition to Jigg's dinner, mustard pickles get put on or alongside a lot of things in Newfoundland: Moose, rabbit, burgers, etc.

Newfoundlanders are SERIOUS about their mustard pickles. In 2016, the main brand available on the island was discontinued, and people lost their minds. It was referred to as "the great pickle crisis" - people rushed to grocers and bought up all they had. Social media was flooded with photos of empty store shelves, there were mustard pickle scalpers, and more. I designed this recipe to be very similar to that original mustard pickle.

Homemade mustard pickles generally use flour, whereas the store-bought source material uses corn starch. Neither is actually recommended for home canning, for various reasons - both safety and performance. So, I'm using a product called "Clear Jel", as I don't want anyone getting botulism! It's a type of specially refined corn starch, specifically designed for this purpose.

Oh, and fair warning: If you're not into sweet pickles, steer clear of this recipe.

Makes about 8 pint jars worth

Fresh cauliflower head	1	1
Pickling cucumbers	3 Lbs	1 ½ kg
Pearl onions	1 lb	500 g
White vinegar	6 cups	1 ½ L
Water	3 cups	750 ml
Granulated sugar	3 2/3 cups	900 ml
Pickling salt	2 Tbsp	30 ml
Mustard powder	6 Tbsp	90 ml
Turmeric powder	1 Tbsp	15 ml
Pickling spice	2 Tbsp	30 ml
Clear Jel	2/3 cup	150 ml

Canning Equipment:

Cheesecloth, twine
Clean, sterilized canning jars & rings
New, never-used, sterilized canning lids
Canning funnel
LARGE pot to process them in
Jar lifter (nice to have, not necessary if you can handle pain!)

Wash all vegetables. Cut cauliflower into bite sized florets, peel the cocktail onions, and slice cucumbers into 3/4-1" thick slices. If you have a wavy slicer, feel free to use that for authenticity!

Fill your LARGE pot with at least 6" of water, put on medium or high heat to bring it to a boil as you prepare your brine.

In another pot (NOT the canning pot!), combine vinegar, water, sugar, salt, mustard powder, and turmeric. Bring to a boil, stirring well to dissolve the salt.

As brine is coming to a boil, cut two large squares from the cheesecloth, stack on top of each other. Measure the pickling spice into the center of the cheesecloth, draw edges of cloth in to enclose the spices, tie into a tight little package with the twine.

Once brine comes to a boil, add spice package and boil for 10-15 minutes, to taste. Once it tastes right to you, remove the spice packet. Add vegetables, stir well, and boil for 10 minutes.

Remove a little of the brine, mix Clear Jel into it until smooth. Add a little more brine if necessary to get it to a pourable consistency, add it all back into the pot and stir well. Boil for 5 more minutes.

After 5 minutes, turn the heat off. Use a sterilized canning funnel and sterilized ladle to scoop pickles and sauce into sterilized canning jars, leaving about 1/2" head space. Wipe off the top edges of the jar with a clean, wet towel, top each with a new, sterilized lid, and carefully screw on a clean lid ring. I like to use a kitchen towel for this, the jars are HOT! Carefully place your jars of pickles into the boiling water pot, allow to process for 15 minutes. CAREFULLY remove them, allow to cool overnight.

The next morning, check to make sure that all of the jars achieved a proper seal – try to push down in the middle of each lid. If it "pops", it did not seal. Any jars that didn't seal should be put in the fridge and used in the next few weeks. Store in a cool, dark area (ideally) for up to 1 year, chill well before eating.

Sweet Mustard Pickles

Salt Beef

I had never heard of salt beef (or "salt meat", "naval beef", the related "Salt riblets", etc) before moving to Newfoundland. In St John's, you can buy salt meat pretty much anywhere, and in many different packaging forms. I've seen it at gas stations and corner stores, in tourist shops, and - of course - in grocery shops. Usually they come in plastic buckets or individually vacuum bagged, but some grocers had it in big vats, where you could select the piece you want, right out of the brine.

Much like Back Bacon (Page 21) and Montreal Smoked Meat (Page 33), Salt meat involves curing the meat for a fairly long time . Generally speaking, the salt meat you buy in stores does NOT indicate the presence of any flavouring - aside from copious amounts of salt - but I like to add a little bit to my brine. Not enough to venture into corned beef territory, mind you... just a little something.

Makes about 4.5 lbs

Beef or pork of choice*	5 lbs	2 ½ kg
Cold water, divided	10 cups	2 ½ L
Pickling salt	1 ½ cups	375 ml
Prague powder #1 cure	2 Tbsp	30 ml
Black peppercorns	1 Tbsp	15 ml
Bay leaves	2	2

Trim most of the visible fat off your meat, if you'd like. Divide meat up between 2 large (gallon) freezer bags.

Measure 2 cups of water into a large pot, add remaining ingredients (aside from meat and rest of water!). Bring to a boil, reduce heat, and simmer for 5 minutes. Remove from heat, add remaining water, stir to combine. Allow to cool to room temperature.

I like to manually divide the pepper corns and bay leaves equally between the two bags before pouring half of the brine into each bag. Push out most of the air, seal the bags, and put them in the fridge – I put both bags into a 9 x 12 cake pan, just in case of leakage, etc. Allow the meat to cure for 8 days, turning once daily to ensure the meat pieces are completely submerged.

After 8 days, discard brine, and rinse meat with cold water. Use paper towels to pat dry. Use right away, or vacuum seal and freeze. Frozen salt meat will taste best if used within 3 months.

To use, follow Jigg's Dinner recipe, page 115. To use on its own: soak in water overnight, then drain. Bring a large pot of water to a boil. Add meat, reduce heat, and simmer gently for 3 hours, or until tender.

* Brisket, riblets, beef navel, etc

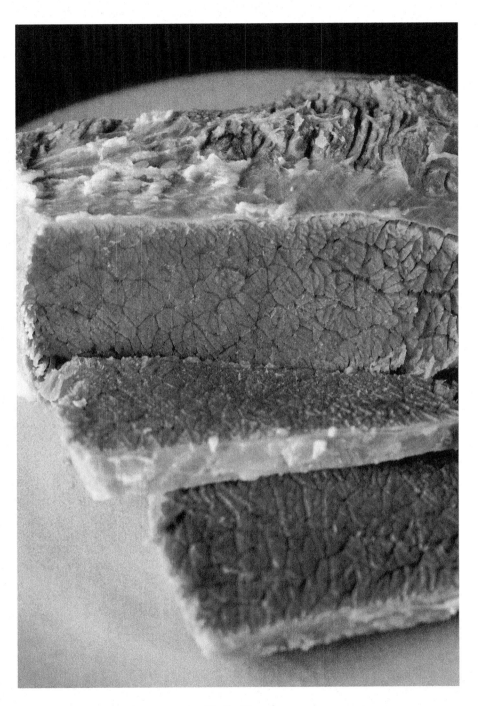

Salt Beef

Pease Pudding

Pease pudding is an incredibly simple thing - basic ingredients, simple process, not a fancy or even pretty final product - but it's an ultimate comfort food. Thick and tasty and warm and satisfying. The fact that it's sort of like the love child of two of my favourite comfort foods - mushy peas and French Canadian Pea Soup (Page 93) certainly doesn't hurt!

Generally speaking - in Newfoundland - pease pudding is made with a pudding bag. This is a plain cotton bag you can buy in any grocery store. Not so common, outside of Newfoundland!

Luckily, cheesecloth works just as well. As a bonus, you can cook up a bigger batch! If I recall correctly, you wouldn't want to use more than a cup or so of peas in a standard pudding bag. You know... BARELY a proper serving! (Yes, I have a problem.)

Makes a big bowl worth

Dried yellow peas	1 lb	500 g
Butter	1/4 cup	50 ml
Salt and pepper		

The night before preparing Jiggs Dinner, place peas in a large bowl, picking out anything that doesn't belong. Cover with warm water, allow to soak overnight, draining the next morning.

In the morning, cut two LARGE squares of cheesecloth, stack on top of each other. Place the soaked peas into the center of the cheesecloth, draw edges of cloth in to enclose the peas. Tie bag off securely with twine, leaving a little head space to allow for expansion. I like to triple knot the twine - if it comes undone, you're going to end up with a really thin pea soup!

Place bag in a large pot of boiling water. Use the ends of the twine - or a separate piece - to tie the twin to the pot handle, to avoid burning it on the bottom of the pan. Be sure to use a long enough tie to allow the peas to rest under the water line.

Boil for 3 hours, replacing water as necessary to keep the peas submerged.

Once it's time to serve, carefully remove the bag from the water, allowing excess water to drain off. Carefully cut the twine, empty bag contents into a serving bowl. Add butter, stirring or mashing until butter is melted and fully incorporated. Season with salt and pepper to taste, serve hot.

Pease Pudding

Newfoundland Style Dressing

There are two big differences between Newfoundland style dressing (stuffing), and the stuffing I grew up with in Winnipeg.

For one, the bread. I was used to torn chunks of bread as the base for the stuffing. In Newfoundland, bread crumbs are used.

Secondly, there's the flavouring. In Winnipeg, most dressing was flavoured with onions, celery, and poultry seasoning. In Newfoundland dressing, you usually skip the celery and any other herbs - besides savoury. It's savoury, or it's not Newfoundland dressing! Don't get fancy with it, you don't need sage or Herbs de Provence or anything - Newfoundland dressing is simple and tasty.

If you can get Mt Scio Savoury, do so! Grown in Newfoundland, it's the standard savoury used there - and for many other Canadian dishes. It also tastes a bit different than the savoury I've been able to purchase in the USA - probably a terroir issue.

If you're not able to get Mt Scio, you're looking for "summer savoury" - not the "winter" variety.

Makes enough to stuff 2 chickens, or 1 turkey

White bread	1 loaf	1 loaf
Medium yellow onion	1	1
Butter	½ cup	125 ml
Dried summer savoury	3-4 Tbsp	45-60 ml
Salt		
Ground black pepper		
Chicken stock		

Tear the bread up into small pieces, then run through a food processor in batches until broken down into crumbs. Place into a large mixing bowl, set aside.

Peel and finely chop onion. In a large pan, saute onion in butter until translucent. Remove onion from heat, add to mixing bowl along with the savoury. Gently stir until well combined, season with salt and pepper to taste.

This can be stuffed into a chicken or turkey as-is, or cooked alongside it in a separate vessel. If cooking separately, add a small amount of chicken stock, mix well, and cover with foil. Bake at 350 for about 25 minutes.

For Gluten-free: Use 2 loaves of your favourite gluten-free bread

Boiled Duff

"Duff" is a boiled or steamed pudding that is quite popular in Newfoundland. It typically comes in two main varieties - Figgy Duff, or Blueberry Duff.

Figgy Duff doesn't actually contain figs - it's a raisin dessert! Apparently - back in the day - raisins were called figs in Newfoundland. Unique? Sure... but if you've ever visited rural Newfoundland, you know that sometimes English words mean very different things in Newfoundland. I say this as someone who uses "I understand people from Upper Island Cove!" as a measure of cred when having certain conversations with Newfoundlanders away.

ANYWAY. "Figgy" is more traditional, while the blueberry version is a popular modern alternative. Blueberry Duff can be made with fresh or frozen blueberries, and can be served either alone, or with caramel sauce. I like to use the same whiskey caramel sauce that I serve with sticky toffee pudding, personally. Figgy duff can also be served alone or with sauce, but the sauce served with it is usually a molasses based one - Molasses Coady - rather than a caramel one.

Generally speaking, Duff is boiled in the same pot as Jiggs Dinner. I do tend to veer off from tradition there, for a couple reasons. For one, I don't like sacrificing pot space that can be used for more potatoes. Secondly, I have horrifically sensitive sense of taste, and can taste the turnips on the pudding when they're boiled together. So, I'll have a separate, smaller pot boiling on the side, just for the duff.

One nice thing about Duffs is that they are endlessly customizable - everyone has their favourite way of making them. Substitute brown sugar or molasses in, add spices and/or orange zest, etc. See the end of the recipe for some suggestions!

Makes 1 large duff - 8 servings or so

All-purpose flour	1 cup	250 ml
Granulated sugar	½ cup	125 ml
Baking powder	1 tsp	5 ml
Salt	1/4 tsp	1 tsp
Butter, melted	1/4 cup	50 ml
Milk	1/3 cup	75 ml
Large egg, beaten	1	1
Blueberries or raisins	1 cup	250 ml

Whisk together dry ingredients. Add butter, milk, and egg, mix just until well incorporated - don't over mix. Gently add blueberries, mix just until distributed.

Scoop dough unto a pudding bag, or into the center of 2 large squares of cheesecloth. Use some twine to tie bag off, leaving 1" of head space for expansion, or gather all of the edges of the cheesecloth and tie securely, allowing a little room for expansion.

Place prepared duff into a pot of gently boiling water. Boil for 1 ½ hours, flipping bag over occasionally.

Once it's time to serve, carefully remove the bag from the water, allowing excess water to drain off. Carefully cut the twine, remove duff from the bag. Place on a serving plate, slice, and serve with sauce of choice.

Variations:

- Add in the zest of one orange or one lemon.

- Add in around 1 tsp of spices, to taste. I like cinnamon and/or cardamom with blueberry duff, or a mix of cinnamon, cloves, and nutmeg with figgy duff.

- Swap packed brown sugar in for the granulated sugar

- Swap 1/4 cup of the sugar for molasses (decrease milk to 1/4 cup for regular, or 1/3 cup for gluten-free)

For Gluten-Free Duff: Increase milk amount to ½ cup, and replace the all-purpose flour with a mixture of ½ cup Sorghum flour, 1/4 cup Coconut flour, 1/4 cup White rice flour, and 1 tsp Xanthan gum

Caramel Sauce for Duff

Butter	1/4 cup	50 ml
Brown sugar, packed	1 1/4 cups	300 ml
Heavy cream	½ cup	125 ml
Rum, brandy, or whiskey, optional	1 Tbsp	15 ml
Vanilla extract	1 tsp	5 ml

Melt butter in a medium saucepan. Add brown sugar and heavy cream, whisking until smooth. Bring to a boil over medium heat, stirring constantly. Boil for 3 minutes - stirring constantly - then remove from heat. Stir in booze of choice - if using - and vanilla. Serve warm, over duff.

Molasses Coady

Butter	1/4 cup	50 ml
Molasses	1 cup	250 ml
Water	1/4 cup	50 ml
White vinegar	1 Tbsp	15 ml

Melt butter in a medium saucepan. Add molasses, water, and vinegar, whisking until smooth. Bring to a boil over medium heat, stirring constantly. Boil for 10 minutes - stirring constantly - then remove from heat. Serve warm, over duff

Boiled Duff

Fries, Dressing, and Gravy

This one isn't so much a recipe, and it's not usually part of Jiggs Dinner... but it is a popular food in Newfoundland - a very common side order or snack food in restaurants, and easily made at home.

Also, leftovers from Jiggs Dinner set you up really nicely to be able to make it... so here we are.

Fries (See page 32)
Leftover dressing
Gravy*

Place freshly cooked fries on a large plate. Sprinkle generously with dressing, top with gravy.

*Leftover gravy from Jiggs Dinner is fine for making this at home, but feel free to use a beef gravy or poutine sauce (page 32), if that's your preference.

Fries, Dressing, & Gravy

Honey Dill Sauce

Condiments and Beverages

Honey Dill Sauce

Honey Dill Sauce is one of those things that I used to think of as being ubiquitous… before moving away from my hometown. When you grow up with something THAT popular, it's weird when you move somewhere that's never even heard of it.

So, let me introduce you to honey dill sauce. This is very much a Winnipeg thing, and "popular" doesn't even begin to describe it. If you order chicken fingers anywhere in Winnipeg, there IS honey dill sauce available. Actually, not even "there IS", more like "There MUST BE". Major chain restaurants, little diners, festival food trucks, school cafeterias… it's just what you do.

I once saw a list of "You know you're from Winnipeg when…", and one of the statements was "You dip everything in Honey Dill sauce". While I wouldn't go so far as to say "everything", it really is a versatile condiment. The most popular use, as I mentioned, is for chicken fingers - both kids and adults love it. It's also great on roasted potato chunks, steamed carrots, salmon, egg rolls, perogies, for crudite plates … and as a french fry dip!

Given that this is a 3 ingredient, "less than 1 minute to make" recipe, I'm a little embarrassed to be starting a chapter off with it. To be fair, this is the very first "Recipe for something I no longer have access to" that I developed, way back when I left Winnipeg for the first time, in 1998. So, I think that earns it a little status, even if it's not anything even approaching haute cuisine.

Makes about 1 cup of sauce

Mayonnaise	2/3 cup	150 ml
Liquid honey	1/3 cup	75 ml
Dried dill weed	1 Tbsp	15 ml

Mix together the mayonnaise and honey until smooth and well blended.

Crush the dried dill weed in your hand (to release more flavour), add to the mayo mixture, stir well.

Cover and refrigerate for at least an hour to allow flavours to blend.

Honey Garlic Sauce

Honey garlic sauce is a popular cooking sauce back home. It's mass produced, super cheap, available everywhere... not healthy at all, but SO tasty. It's also one of the most popular flavours for wings pretty much anywhere I've been in Canada, while not so much of a thing in the USA.

This recipe was developed several years ago, inspired by a fellow Canadian expat's tweet, which bemoaned the lack of honey garlic sauce available where she was. A ridiculous amount of math and problem solving ensued, and I soon ended up creating this very accurate re-creation. On first taste, it hit my memory *just* right, and I was transported back to my apartment, circa my early 20s. It took me back to quick stir fry meals thrown together cheaply and easily, when I bothered to take the time to eat. I was SO busy back then, I'd sew for 16+ hours in a day, skipping meals often. Convenience foods like these bottled sauces were go-to meals, as I had NO time to "properly" cook.

This is not high cuisine, and I have NO idea how it would fit on the American palate – us Canadians tend to have a ridiculous sweet tooth! Who knows - maybe there's a reason it hasn't caught on in the USA! For an ex-pat Canadian, though... the nostalgia that this food evokes brings it to "comfort food" levels, even as a condiment. Isn't taste-memory a funny thing?

This sauce is great as a stir fry sauce, or to cook meatballs or spare ribs in. For our first use of it, we simply browned some pork chops, added sliced peppers to the pan, and cooked it for a few minutes. Then we added about 3/4 cup of the sauce and let it cook a few more minutes, and served over rice. Fabulous!

Makes about 2 cups

Granulated sugar	1 cup	250 ml
Water	2/3 cup	150 ml
Liquid honey	½ cup	125 ml
Molasses	1/4 cup	50 ml
Salt	1 tsp	5 ml
Lemon juice	1 tsp	5 ml
Garlic cloves, pressed or minced	8-10	8-10
Corn starch	1 tsp	5 ml

Combine sugar, 1/3 cup of the water, honey, molasses, salt, lemon juice, and garlic in a saucepan. Heat to a boil, stirring well to dissolve and combine ingredients. Once mixture boils, turn heat down and simmer for 5 minutes.

Whisk corn starch into remaining 1/3 cup of water, add to saucepan. Stir until well incorporated and cook until mixture starts to thicken. Remove from heat. Strain garlic out, if you'd like - I don't tend to, but it's totally up to you. If not using the sauce right away, transfer to a clean mason jar, cover, and refrigerate for use within two weeks.

Honey Garlic Sauce

Rotisserie Chicken Sauce

... AKA "Crack Sauce".

The source material for this recipe is served at a popular restaurant chain in Canada, as an accompaniment to a chicken dinner. You're meant to dip pieces of rotisserie chicken in it.. but I know plenty of people from back home who will straight up drink any that remains after dinner - myself included!

Packets of an instant version are available at grocery stores in Canada - a popular item for expats on vacation to bring home - but it's not the same. I always assumed that the sauce was made from ingredients like chicken broth, tomato juice, etc... but as it turns out, the restaurants also make them from a dry mix.

As no one wants to fuss with shopping for tomato powder and dried chicken fat, this homemade version goes in the direction of my original assumption, rather than sticking to "this is how they do it". I had a container of straight-from-the-restaurant sauce on hand as I fussed with ingredients and amounts - so this was fun to develop - it is VERY close to the source material!

Makes about 3 ½ cups

Butter	4 Tbsp	60 ml
Corn starch	3 Tbsp	45 ml
Chicken broth	3 cups	750 ml
Tomato juice	1/4 cup	50 ml
White vinegar	1 tsp	5 ml
Onion powder	1 ½ tsp	7 ml
Paprika	1 ½ tsp	7 ml
Dried sage	3/4 tsp	3 ml
Garlic powder	½ tsp	2 ml
Salt	½ tsp	2 ml
Dried summer savoury	½ tsp	2 ml
Ginger powder	1/4 tsp	1 ml
Mustard powder	1/4 tsp	1 ml
Thyme	1/4 tsp	1 ml
Bay leaf	1	1

In a medium sized saucepan, melt butter over medium heat. Allow to cook, whisking frequently, until it just starts to brown a little.. Add corn starch, whisk until smooth. Add chicken broth a little at a time, whisking to fully incorporate butter mixture.

Add remaining ingredients, whisk well. Turn heat up to medium-high, bring just to a boil. Turn heat down to low and simmer for 5 minutes. Remove bay leaf, serve hot.

Rotisserie Chicken Sauce

Plum Sauce

Plum sauce is a popular condiment back home, produced by the same company who puts out the Honey Garlic Sauce - and others.

The source material involves a base of pumpkin puree, where many commercially available plum sauces outside of Canada don't contain any pumpkin at all. While all-plum plum sauce is going to be higher quality, in general... sometimes you just want what you're used to. "Canadian style plum sauce" was a frequent request when it came to polling about what belongs in this book!

My recipe diverges slightly from source material in that I skipped the trace amounts of tomato and molasses - they just weren't necessary, and over-complicated things.

This is a nice, clean tasting sauce. Very close to the source material, but fresher tasting. It's great as a dip for egg rolls, chicken fingers, spring rolls, etc.

Makes about 1 cup

Plums	2	2
White vinegar	1/3 cup	75 ml
Granulated sugar	1/3 cup	75 ml
Pumpkin puree	1/4 cup	50 ml
Corn starch	1 Tbsp	15 ml
Lemon juice	2 tsp	10 ml
Crushed chilies / red pepper flakes	1/4 tsp	1 ml
Garlic powder	1/4 tsp	1 ml
Ginger powder	1/4 tsp	1 ml
Salt and pepper, optional		

Peel and chop plums, discard pits. Add plums to a food processor or blender along with remaining ingredients - except salt and pepper - process until very smooth.

Strain mixture through a wire strainer, stirring until only dry solids remain. Discard solids.

Transfer plum mixture to a medium saucepan, Bring to a boil, turn heat down to low, and gently simmer for 2 minutes.

Remove from heat, cool to room temperature. Season with salt and pepper to taste, cover, and chill until use.

Plum Sauce

Cherry Sauce

Cherry sauce is the Canadian version of the red "sweet and sour sauce" that is served alongside chicken balls or fried shrimp in Asian restaurants in the USA. The American version lacking flavour or "not tasting right" is a common complaint among Canadian expats, so here it is!

The use of tart cherry extract is due to the fairly widespread availability of that ingredient. If you would prefer to use pure or reconstituted cherry juice, use 3/4 cup of it, and omit both the water and tart cherry concentrate. Also note: The use of real cherry juice gives this a more natural colour, rather than the bright, fake cherry red that the source material features. Sorry about that!

Makes about 1 ½ cups

Cold water	½ cup	125 ml
Granulated sugar	½ cup	125 ml
White vinegar	1/3 cup	75 ml
Tart cherry concentrate	1/4 cup	50 ml
Corn starch	4 tsp	20 ml
Lemon juice	1 tsp	5 ml
Salt	1/4 tsp	1 ml

In a small saucepan, whisk all ingredients together, bring to a boil over medium heat. Once boiling, turn heat off and allow to simmer - whisking constantly - for one minute, or until it thickens.

Remove from heat, cool to room temperature. Transfer to appropriate bottle or jar, chill until use.

Cherry Sauce

139

"Artemis" Sauces

This group of recipes are all based on a line of BBQ sauces that are very popular in Canada - and one of the items frequently featured in "look what I brought back!" brag posts on Canadian expat forums. I've renamed them for this book, but very accurately reproduced all of the flavours from that line. The main recipe here is for "Original", and the variations to create all 6 of the other flavours follow.

Makes about 2 cups

Canned tomato puree	1 cup	250 ml
Granulated sugar	1 cup	250 ml
White vinegar	3/4 cup	175 ml
Dijon mustard	1 Tbsp	15 ml
Molasses	1 Tbsp	15 ml
Garlic powder	1 tsp	5 ml
Worcestershire sauce	1 tsp	5 ml
Onion powder	½ tsp	2 ml
Paprika	½ tsp	2 ml
Salt	½ tsp	2 ml
Turmeric	½ tsp	2 ml
Cayenne powder	1/4 tsp	1 ml
Ground black pepper	1/4 tsp	1 ml

In a medium saucepan, whisk together all ingredients. Bring to a boil, reduce heat and simmer 5 minutes. Cool, transfer to storage container, and chill until use.

Chicken and Rib Sauce: Add ½ tsp dried sage and a pinch of thyme.

Gourmet Spicy Sauce: Increase cayenne powder to ½ tsp, add ½ tsp chili powder.

Honey Dijon Sauce: Decrease granulated sugar to ½ cup, and turmeric to 1/4 tsp. Omit white vinegar. Add ½ cup liquid honey and ½ cup cider vinegar. Increase Dijon mustard to 1/4 cup.

Honey Garlic Sauce: Decrease granulated sugar to ½ cup, and turmeric to 1/4 tsp. Add ½ cup liquid honey. Increase garlic powder to 2 tsp, and salt to 3/4 tsp.

Maple Sauce: Decrease granulated sugar to 1/4 cup, and turmeric to 1/4 tsp. Add 1 cup dark or B grade (if available) maple syrup

Smokehouse Sauce: Increase molasses to 1/4 cup, and salt to 3/4 tsp. Decrease turmeric to 1/4 tsp. Add 5 tsp liquid smoke and 1/4 tsp chili powder.

"Artemis" Sauces

"Artemis" Garlic & Herb Marinade

This is a replica of a popular store-bought marinade back home, from the same producer of the BBQ sauces from page 140.

This marinade goes particularly well on chicken, fish, and vegetables.

Makes about 1 1/4 cups marinade.

White vinegar	3/4 cup	175 ml
Vegetable oil	1/4 cup	50 ml
Water	1/4 cup	50 ml
Granulated sugar	3 Tbsp	45 ml
Dried oregano	2 ½ tsp	12 ml
Salt	2 ½ tsp	12 ml
Dried parsley	2 tsp	10 ml
Corn starch	1 ½ tsp	7 ml
Fresh lemon zest	1 tsp	5 ml
Garlic powder	1 tsp	5 ml
Thyme	3/4 tsp	3 ml
Dried basil	½ tsp	2 ml
Onion powder	½ tsp	2 ml
Paprika	1/4 tsp	1 ml
Rosemary	1/4 tsp	1 ml
Cayenne powder	1/8 tsp	½ ml
Garlic cloves, pressed	5	5

Whisk all ingredients together in a small sauce pan. Bring to just a simmer over medium heat. Remove from heat and cool before using.

To use, marinate food items for about 30 minutes, before cooking.

"Artemis" Garlic & Herb Marinade

"Artemis" Montreal Steak Spice Marinade

Much like the garlic and herb marinade, the source material for this is a popular, commercially available product in Canada. It's particularly good for steak and vegetables. If using commercial steak spice, leave out the ½ tsp salt. Taste, add more salt if necessary. To make this gluten-free, be sure to use a gluten-free soy sauce.

Makes about 1 1/4 cups marinade.

White vinegar	½ cup	125 ml
Vegetable oil	1/4 cup	50 ml
Water	1/4 cup	50 ml
Granulated sugar	3 Tbsp	45 ml
Montreal steak spice (Recipe below)	2 Tbsp	30 ml
Corn starch	1 tsp	5 ml
Mustard powder	1 tsp	5 ml
Soy sauce	1 tsp	5 ml
Paprika	½ tsp	2 ml
Salt	½ tsp	2 ml
Thyme	1/4 tsp	1 ml

Whisk all ingredients together in a small sauce pan. Bring to just a simmer over medium heat. Remove from heat and cool before using. To use, marinate food items for about 30 minutes, before cooking.

Montreal Steak Spice

A homemade version of a store bought favourite... and it will ruin you for the source material! Makes about ½ cup.

Black peppercorns	2 Tbsp	30 ml
Dried minced garlic	1 ½ Tbsp	25 ml
Coriander seeds	2 tsp	10 ml
Dill Seed	2 tsp	10 ml
Crushed chilies / red pepper flakes	1 ½ tsp	7 ml
Salt	1 Tbsp	15 ml
Onion powder	1 tsp	5 ml
Paprika	½ tsp	2 ml

Measure peppercorns, garlic, coriander, dill, and pepper flakes into a nonstick pan. Toast over medium high heat - stirring constantly - until fragrant. Remove from heat, allow to cool. Transfer toasted spices to a small food processor or spice grinder, blitz until ingredients are fairly fine, but still mostly identifiable. Mix in remaining ingredients. Store in an airtight container.

Montreal Steak Spice, "Artemis" Steak Spice Marinade

All Dressed, Dill Pickle, and Ketchup Seasonings

Popcorn Seasonings

I designed these seasonings as a replicas for the most popular chip flavours in Canada. You can use these on popcorn, chips, fries, baked potatoes, meats.. One friend loves the all-dressed on mac and cheese! For each flavour, combine all ingredients, and store in an air tight container.

All Dressed Seasoning - Makes about a cup

Vinegar powder	1/3 cup	75 ml
Tomato powder	2 Tbsp	30 ml
Salt	2 Tbsp	30 ml
Brown sugar, packed	1 ½ Tbsp	25 ml
Sour cream powder	2 tsp	10 ml
Garlic powder	1 tsp	5 ml
Nutritional yeast	1 tsp	5 ml
Onion powder	1 tsp	5 ml
Smoked paprika	1 tsp	5 ml
Citric acid	3/4 tsp	3 ml
Allspice	1/4 tsp	1 ml
Celery seed	1/4 tsp	1 ml
Cloves	1/4 tsp	1 ml
Ground black pepper	1/4 tsp	1 ml
Mustard powder	1/4 tsp	1 ml

Dill Pickle Seasoning - Makes about 3/4 cups

Vinegar powder	½ cup	125 ml
Dill weed	1/3 cup	75 ml
Salt	1/4 cup	50 ml
Mustard powder	3/4 tsp	3 ml
Garlic powder	1/4- ½ tsp	1-2 ml
Ground black pepper	1/4- ½ tsp	1-2 ml

Ketchup Seasoning - Makes about 3/4 cup

Tomato powder	1/3 cup	75 ml
Vinegar Powder	4 Tbsp	60 ml
Salt	2 Tbsp	30 ml
Sugar	1 Tbsp	15 ml
Paprika	½ tsp	2 ml
Allspice	1/4 tsp	1 ml
Garlic powder	1/4 tsp	1 ml
Onion Powder	1/4 tsp	1 ml
Celery seed	1/8 tsp	½ ml
Cloves	1/8 tsp	½ ml

Ketchup Aux Fruits

Not the smooth ketchup you're used to on an average hotdog, Ketchup Aux Fruits is a fruit based relish, a popular condiment in Quebec. It's a great accompaniment to Tourtière, with meats, on shepherd's pie, and as a relish on cheese trays, with sandwich meats and bread

Makes about 12 cups, depending on how watery tomatoes are, etc

Large red tomatoes	12	12
Large yellow onions	2	2
Apples	2	2
Pears	2	2
Peaches	2	2
Green bell pepper	1	1
Red bell pepper	1	1
Celery ribs, chopped	2	2
Apple cider vinegar	2 cups	500 ml
Granulated sugar	2 cups	500 ml
Canning salt	1 Tbsp	15 ml
Pickling spices	1/4 cup	50 ml

Blanch tomatoes: Add to a pot of boiling water, boil for 2 minutes. Strain tomatoes out of boiling water, add to a bowl of ice water to stop cooking. Strain when cool, peel skins off all tomatoes.

Peel onions, apples, pears, and peaches, seed peppers. Chop tomatoes, onions, fruits, peppers, and celery into small, uniformly sized pieces. Place fruits and vegetables into a large pot, along with vinegar, sugar, and salt. Stir well.

Measure pickling spice onto a doubled-over piece of cheese cloth, gather edges and use a small piece of twine to secure into a little package; add to pot. Bring mixture to a rolling boil, reduce heat to simmer. Simmer, stirring occasionally, until mixture is thick - about 1.5 - 2 hours. Remove spice packet, squeezing excess liquid back into the pot.

Use a sterilized canning funnel and sterilized ladle to scoop ketchup into sterilized canning jars, leaving about 1/8" head space. Wipe off the top edges of the jar with a clean, wet towel, top each with a new, sterilized lid, and carefully screw on a clean lid ring. I like to use a kitchen towel for this, the jars are HOT! Carefully place your jars of relish into the boiling water pot, allow to process for 15 minutes. CAREFULLY remove them, allow to cool overnight.

The next morning, check to make sure that all of the jars achieved a proper seal – try to push down in the middle of each lid. If it "pops", it did not seal. Any jars that didn't seal should be put in the fridge and used in the next few weeks. Store in a cool, dark area (ideally) for up to 1 year, chill well before eating.

Ketchup Aux Fruits

Chow Chow

This maritime relish is most popular in Nova Scotia, but can also be found in Quebec, where it's a bit less sweet, and referred to as "green tomato ketchup". It can be used on Tourtière, on french fries, with hamburgers, on bread, with vegetables, etc. It can be used to brighten up almost any basic meat, including chicken, pork, and fish. This recipe can easily be doubled, if you know you'll use a lot! 6 lbs of green tomatoes usually works out to about 6 large tomatoes.

Makes about 8 cups, or 4 pints

Fresh green tomatoes	6 lbs	1 ½ kg
Large yellow or white onions	2	2
Chopped celery	4 cups	1000 ml
Green bell peppers	2	2
Pickling salt	½ cup	125 ml
Granulated sugar	3 cups	750 ml
White vinegar	2 cup	500 ml
Pickling spices	3 Tbsp	45 ml
Mustard powder	1/4 tsp	1 ml
Turmeric	1/4 tsp	1 ml

Thinly slice tomatoes and onions, toss with pickling salt, leave overnight. Drain excess liquid.

Place drained vegetables in a large pot, along with sugar and vinegar.

Measure pickling spice onto a doubled-over piece of cheese cloth, gather edges and use a small piece of twine to secure into a little package; add to pot, along with turmeric and mustard powder. Bring mixture to a rolling boil, reduce heat to simmer. Simmer, stirring occasionally, until mixture is thick - 20 minutes. Remove spice packet, squeezing excess liquid back into the pot.

Use a sterilized canning funnel and sterilized ladle to scoop Chow Chow into sterilized canning jars, leaving about 1/8" head space. Wipe off the top edges of the jar with a clean, wet towel, top each with a new, sterilized lid, and carefully screw on a clean lid ring. I like to use a kitchen towel for this, the jars are HOT! Carefully place your jars of relish into the boiling water pot, allow to process for 20 minutes. CAREFULLY remove them, allow to cool overnight.

The next morning, check to make sure that all of the jars achieved a proper seal – try to push down in the middle of each lid. If it "pops", it did not seal. Any jars that didn't seal should be put in the fridge and used in the next few weeks. Store in a cool, dark area (ideally) for up to 1 year, chill well before eating.

Chow Chow

"Honk"

Ah, ... "Honk". Yes, let's call this "Honk"... I didn't know it was specific to Canada when I was growing up, or that it was *HIGHLY* regional within Canada - put out by a Nova Scotia Dairy, but licensed out to other dairies for production. I just knew that it was a fun tasting "juice", and that it basically tasted like childhood.

It came about in the 1960s, was served at Canadian breakfasts and in Canadian lunch boxes for decades, then was discontinued in 2010. People lost their minds, started up campaigns, and eventually it was brought back in 2012... but then discontinued again in 2015. RIP, "Honk"!

I had a bunch of requests for coming up for a recipe for "Honk", and on the surface, I thought it would be relatively easy - it's just a juice blend, right? Well, the lack of source material is one obstacle (though nostalgia memory can be reliable once I get close to the right mix!)... but then there's the issue of source material ingredients.

... I had no idea that it was only 25% juice, or that it contained both canola oil and modified corn starch. Bizarre!

So, while I can't bring myself to design a recipe for a juice drink that includes oil and modified corn starch in it (ick), I CAN put together a juice blend that tastes extremely similar, and will definitely scratch that itch.

I'm including citric acid in place of ascorbic acid (vitamin C), as it's a more common kitchen ingredient. This brightens the taste up, but isn't necessary, if you don't already have some on hand.

Makes about 1L

Water	2 cups	500 ml
Granulated sugar	2/3 cup	150 ml
Citric acid (optional)	½ tsp	2 ml
Orange Juice	½ cup	125 ml
Apple juice	1/3 cup	75 ml
Apricot nectar	1/3 cup	75 ml
Pineapple juice	2 Tbsp	30 ml
Prune juice	2 Tbsp	30 ml

Measure water, sugar, and citric acid (if using) together in a small saucepan. Bring to a boil, stirring until sugar is dissolved. Remove from heat, allow to cool.

In a large beverage container (1L or more), mix remaining ingredients. Add sugar syrup, stir well to combine. Chill until use, shake/stir before serving.

"Honk"

Butter Tart Liqueur

A while back, I was craving butter tarts . That's nothing new, as a Canadian away from home – I'm always craving something that I either can't get at all, or will have to make myself.

What was new is that I was drinking at the time, (Ok, THAT part isn't new!)... and got it in my head that "Butter tart" would make a lovely flavour for a liqueur or cocktail. I immediately set about working through some ideas, deciding which way would be best to go.

In the end, doing a custom infused spirit and then turning it into a liqueur made the most sense.

This takes very little in the way of ingredients or effort, and the result will make any butter tart fan – or general Sweet Tooth – very happy!

Makes about 6 cups

Dark raisins	1 cup	250 ml
Vanilla beans	2	2
Decent quality vodka	3 cups	750 ml
Brown sugar, packed	2 ½ cups	625 ml
Maple syrup	½ cup	125 ml
Water	½ cup	125 ml

Place raisins in a large, clean jar.

Slice vanilla beans lengthwise, scoop the seeds out. Add beans and seeds to the jar, top with vodka, and shake well. Store in a cool, dark place for about 4-7 days, shaking daily.

After a few days, taste. If the flavour is good and strong (it'll likely be!), strain out raisins and vanilla, discard.* If you want more flavour, allow it to sit for another week or so, shaking daily.

Combine brown sugar, maple syrup, and water in a pot. Cook over medium heat, stirring frequently, until sugar is fully dissolved. Remove from heat, allow to cool. Combine infused vodka with maple-brown sugar syrup, stirring or shaking well to combine. Bottle in clean wine or liqueur bottles.

After bottling, you should let it age for about a week in a cool place before drinking it – IF you have that kind of patience! Aging results in a smoother, more mellow flavour.

* Saving a few vodka raisins to place in the liqueur bottle makes for a cute presentation idea.

Butter Tart Liqueur

Maple Liqueur

Maple Liqueur

Maple liqueur can be as simple or as complex as you would like it to be. At the very minimum, you'll need a spirit, water, and maple syrup. The spirit can be neutral - like vodka - or something with a bit more flavour, like rum or brandy.

However, if you infuse your spirit before mixing your liqueur ingredients, you can come up with far more depth of flavour. Rather than straight maple, you can add spices, herbs, and/or fruit peel - alone or in combination - to really compliment the base maple flavour. I'm personally a fan of steeping orange peel, a split vanilla bean, and a cinnamon stick in vodka or brandy, and using that infusion as the base for my maple liqueur. Have fun with it!

Basic Maple Liqueur

Maple syrup	1 part	1 part
Water	1 part	1 part
Spirit of choice	1-2 parts	1-2 parts

Combine maple syrup and water in a saucepan. Heat to a simmer, stirring until syrup is dissolved. Remove from heat and cool to room temperature.

Add 1 part of spirit to maple syrup mixture, taste. Add more spirit, a little at a time, if desired. Transfer to a clean bottle, cover, and allow to age for about 1 month in the fridge before drinking - IF you have that kind of patience.

Infusing Spirits for Maple Liqueur

- Start by choosing the flavour you'd like. If using more than one flavour, what kind of proportions do you want? The next consideration is the spirit that you will be infusing. Think about the flavour of the spirit, the flavour you'll be infusing... and also about the final intended use of your infused spirit.

- If you're looking to really showcase the flavour of the maple syrup and flavourings you add, you'll want to choose a spirit that is fairly light, and possibly neutral. Vodka works beautifully for almost any flavour, and rum works well with maple, without overpowering it.

- Brandy and whisky can also be used, but because they have big flavour on their own, you'll want to plan around that. Either plan for a brandy or whiskey with just a hint of flavour infused, or pick big, robust flavours to infuse.

- If your infusion lacks flavour even after steeping for a couple of weeks, just add more of your flavouring agents, and continue infusing until it's just right!

- If your infusion has too strong of a flavour after steeping, just add a little more spirit, to taste. Allowing infusion to age is important in this case! Remember, you'll be adding water and maple syrup after infusing, which will dilute the infusion flavour by about 50%.

- The more surface area, the easier the flavour will extract. For this reason, you'll want to chop large pieces into smaller chunks.

To infuse spirits:

- Place all ingredients into a large, clean mason jar, cap tightly.
- Shake filled jars a few times every day during the infusion process.
- Taste for doneness.
- Once desired flavour strength is achieved, strain the infused spirit first with a fine mesh strainer, then a second time through a coffee filter. Transfer strained liqueur to clean bottles/jars for storage.

For 3 cups of spirit, use the following table to determine amount of ingredients, and recommended infusion time.

	Amount needed	Infusion Time
Fruits	1 - 1 ½ cups / 250-375 ml	1 week: Citrus fruits 2 weeks: Berries, cherries 3 weeks: Apples, pears, stone fruits
Fresh Herbs	½ cup / 125 ml	Allow to infuse for approximately 3-5 days, tasting daily.
Spices	2-3 Tbsp / 30-45 ml	Allow to infuse for approximately 2-5 days, tasting daily.
Coffee Beans	½ cup / 125 ml	Allow to infuse for approximately 5 days.
Vanilla Bean	1-2 beans, split	Allow to infuse for 2 weeks, minimum

Fruits: Prepare fruit before using:

Wash, leave peels on, chop: Citrus fruits
Wash, chop, slice, and/or lightly mash: Berries
Wash, remove pit/core, chop fruit: Apples, cherries, stone fruits

158

<u>Herbs:</u> Use clean, fresh herbs, like rosemary, Mint, Basil, Etc

<u>Spices:</u> Use whole dry spices, such as star anise, cinnamon sticks, cardamom pods, whole nutmeg, etc. If using something really pungent, like peppercorns, start with a smaller amount - even ½ tsp

Maple Creme Liqueur Recipe

Maple syrup	1 part	1 part
Condensed milk	1 part	1 part
Infused (or not) spirit of choice	1 ½ parts	1 ½ parts
Chocolate, chopped (optional)		

Combine heavy cream and sweetened condensed milk in a saucepan. Heat to a simmer, stirring constantly. If adding chocolate (as much or as little as you want), mix in at this point, stirring until melted and completely incorporated into cream. Remove from heat, allow to cool.

In a blender, mixer, or food processor, blend cooled milk mixture with infused spirit. Beat/blend on high for about 2 minutes to emulsify the mixture. Bottle, store in fridge. Use within 1 month, giving bottle a good shake if any separation has occurred

Caribou

Caribou

My first exposure to Caribou - as a Winnipegger - came through the French Canadian pavilion at Folklorama. There, it was served room temperature, alongside many other French Canadian specialties. Aside from Folkorama, it's also commonly served at other French Canadian cultural events, both inside Quebec (Carnival, sugar shacks, winter parades, winter sporting events, etc), and outside (Like Festival du Voyageur, also in Winnipeg). During Carnival in Quebec, it's commonly served in long, hollow plastic canes, capped off with a Bonhomme head - Bonhomme being the snowman mascot of the event.

They say that it was customary - way back in the day - for fur trappers to drink the warm blood of freshly hunted caribou, and would mix it with alcohol. This was apparently both for energy, and to keep warm. As time went on, the blood was replaced with wine, but the name remained.

You can buy premade Caribou in Canadian liquor stores these days, but it's always nicer when you make it yourself. Because Caribou is so highly customizable, this is one of those non-recipe recipes - more a set of guidelines, than anything.

In general:

- Proportions tend to be about 1 part hard alcohol to 3 parts wine, but you can make it weaker or stronger as desired.

- You can serve it warmed, room temperature, or chilled. At some events, it's served out of shot glasses made of ice!

- You can use any red wine you like. You can swap all or part of the red wine for sherry or port, if desired

- You can serve it as a mixed cocktail, or as a mulled drink served from a crockpot.

- You have some wiggle room on the hard alcohol, too. Whiskey is most common, but rum, brandy, and/or vodka are acceptable substitutes.

- Sweetener can be either maple syrup (traditional, recommended!), or sugar. The amount depends on the sweetness of the wine used, and personal taste.

- It's considered good form to use Canadian wine and liquor wherever possible :)

Cold or Room Temperature Caribou

Hard alcohol of choice	1 part	1 part
Red wine of choice	2-3 parts	2-3 parts
Maple syrup or sugar		
Cloves, nutmeg, and/or cinnamon (Optional)		

Mix together alcohol and wine. Add maple syrup - or sugar - to taste. Add a pinch of spice(s), if desired, stir well.

Drink right away, chill, or pour into a wine bottle, Mason jar, or other appropriate vessel. Seal, and allow to "age" for a couple weeks before serving.

Mulled Caribou

Hard alcohol of choice	1 part	1 part
Red wine of choice	2-3 parts	2-3 parts
Maple syrup or sugar		

Optional additions: Orange slices, orange or lemon peel, whole cloves, cinnamon sticks, grated nutmeg, dried cranberries,

In a medium saucepan or crock pot, mix together alcohol and red wine. Add maple syrup - or sugar - to taste, stir well. Heat until steaming - not simmering or boiling - and serve hot.

Partridgeberry Wine

Partridgeberries are indigenous to Newfoundland, as well as Scandinavia. They're tart little red berries that taste like a cross between a cranberry and a blueberry… you may know them as "lingonberries", if you're a fan of IKEA!

They are one of a few amazing berries that grow wild in Newfoundland; they're very popular in Newfoundland cuisine, appearing in jams, sauces, in candies, on cheesecake… and in wine. You can buy partridgeberry wine in local wine stores back home, as there are several Newfoundland wineries that specialize in it. Great as-is, it was also my secret ingredient in moose stew!

Unfortunately, you can't buy partridgeberry wine here in Minnesota - or anywhere else that I've seen, outside of Canada. Homesick desperation is one of the mothers of invention in my kitchen, and a few years ago I created a recipe for partridgeberry wine when were able to buy a case of the berries from a local wholesaler!

This makes a full bodied, gorgeous wine. It's a fairly sweet wine, with a great mouth feel .. very delicious, and very luxurious. Definitely worth the effort of finding a case of partridgeberries!

If you haven't attempted making wine before, don't be intimidated! Check out our primer to home brewing on my "Celebration Generation" blog - the address is in the Resources section, Page 229. Just a small handful of entries to read, and you'll be good to go!

Unable to get your hands on partridgeberries? I actually designed a "faux partridgeberry" wine recipe, which you can find on page 166!

Makes about 5 gallons

Frozen partridgeberries	15 lbs	6.75 kg
Granulated sugar	13 lbs	6 kg
Bottled spring water	5 gallons	19 L
Acid blend	2 ½ tsp	12 ml
Pectic enzyme	2 ½ tsp	12 ml
Tannin	1 1/4 tsp	6 ml
Yeast nutrient	1 tsp	5 ml
Golden raisins	5 lbs	2 kg
Red Star Montrechet wine yeast	2 packets	2 packets
Wine stabilizer of choice		

Allow the partridgeberries to partially thaw, then coarsely chop them (A food processor comes in handy!). Place berries and sugar into a large (7+ gallon) pot, stir until well combined. Add water, stir well to dissolve sugar.

Heat to ALMOST boiling – stirring constantly – then simmer gently for 10 minutes. Stir in acid blend, enzyme, tannin, nutrient, and raisins.

Pour mixture into a freshly sanitized 6.5 gallon fermenting bucket. Cover with sanitized lid and air lock, allow to cool to room temperature (overnight).

The next morning, give the mixture a quick stir with a long, sanitized spoon, and – using sanitized equipment – take a gravity reading. Keep track of the number! (This is an optional step, but will allow you to calculate your final ABV % - See "Resources", page 229)

Sprinkle yeast into fermenter, cover with sanitized cover and air lock. Within 48 hours, you should notice fermentation activity – bubbles in the airlock, carbonation and /or swirling in the wine must. This means you're good to go!

After a week or so, use your sanitized siphon setup to rack the liquid into a freshly sanitized 6- 6.5 gallon carboy, discarding the berry pulp.

Leave the carboy in a cool dark place to do its thing for a month or so.

Using sanitized equipment, rack the partridgeberry wine off the sediment, into a clean, freshly sanitized 5 or 6 gallon carboy. Cap with sanitized airlock, leave it alone for another 2-3 months.

Rack one more time, leave it for another 3 months or so.

When your wine has been racked a few times and shows NO more fermenting activity for a month or so (no bubbles in the airlock, no more sediment being produced), you can move on to bottling.

Follow the instructions on your selected type of wine stabilizer to stop fermentation. For potassium sorbate, this needs to be done 2-3 days before bottling.

Using sanitized equipment, take a final gravity reading, then rack the wine into clean, sanitized bottles. Cork, and store in a cool, dry place until use.

We like to use "Zorks" for corking our homemade wine. Easy to use – no special equipment needed! – easy to uncork, and – should you have any wine left in your bottle after serving - the "cork" is easily replaced for temporary storage

Partridgeberry Wine & Faux Partridgeberry Wine

Faux Partridgeberry Wine

While living in Newfoundland - Though I'd never been a fan of red GRAPE wines - Partridgeberry wine became a fast favourite for me. Not only was it great for drinking, it was a favourite ingredient for cooking wild game. It was one of 2 secret ingredients in my moose stew. Oh, yum. It's been far too long… Anyway.

A year or two after making my first batch of partridgeberry wine, I went to place another order, and was told that they wouldn't be able to stock it that year. Apparently it had been a lighter crop, and there was slim availability for wholesale in the USA. So, I worked up a "Plan B" – I created a "Faux Partridgeberry" wine!

Using the "like a cranberry crossed with a blueberry" flavour profile, I experimented with proportions, and came up with a VERY passable "partridgeberry" wine. The colour was only slightly different from the original thing, and the flavour is SO close, it'd fool most partridgeberry fans. Oh, this is good stuff! While this recipe is for a 1 gallon batch, you can very easily multiply the ingredients to make a larger, 5 or 6 gallon batch!

If you haven't attempted making wine before, don't be intimidated! Check out our primer to home brewing on my "Celebration Generation" blog - the address is in the Resources section, Page 229. Just a small handful of entries to read, and you'll be good to go!

Makes slightly less than 1 gallon of finished wine

Frozen blueberries	12 oz	340 g
Frozen cranberries	10 oz	300 g
Granulated sugar	3 lbs	1 ½ kg
White grape juice concentrate	1 can	1 can
Bottled spring water	1 gallon	4 L
Acid blend	1 tsp	5 ml
Pectic enzyme	1/4 tsp	1 ml
Yeast nutrient	1 tsp	5 ml
Red Star Montrachet wine yeast	1 packet	1 packet
Wine stabilizer of choice		

Equipment needed:

2 gallon pot
One 1.5 gallon fermenter bucket and lid
Two 1 gallon glass carboys & stoppers
1 air lock
Hydrometer, optional
Siphon, siphon tubing

Allow the blueberries and cranberries to thaw. Puree until thick but runny. Strain juice into a large pot, reserving the berry pulp. (Best to put the strainer/colander onto a plate, in the meantime.)

Add sugar and grape juice concentrate to the pot, stir until well combined. Add water to just over 1 gallon of total liquid. Once you've added enough water, add the berry pulp back into the pot. Heat to ALMOST boiling, then simmer gently for 10 minutes. Stir in acid blend, enzyme, and nutrient.

Pour mixture into a freshly sanitized 1.5 gallon fermenting bucket. Cover with sanitized lid and air lock, allow to cool to room temperature (overnight).

The next morning, give the mixture a quick stir with a sanitized spoon, and – using sanitized equipment – take a gravity reading. Keep track of the number! (This is an optional step, but will allow you to calculate your final ABV % - See "Resources", page 229)

Sprinkle yeast into fermenter, cover with sanitized cover and air lock. Within 48 hours, you should notice fermentation activity – bubbles in the airlock, carbonation and /or swirling in the wine must. This means you're good to go!

After a week or so, use your sanitized siphon setup to rack the liquid into a freshly sanitized 1 gallon carboy. Discard the pulp, and leave the carboy in a cool dark place to do its thing for a month or so.

Using sanitized equipment, rack the lingonberry wine off the sediment, into a clean, freshly sanitized 1 gallon carboy. Cap with sanitized airlock, leave it alone for another 2-3 months.

Rack one more time, leave it for another 3 months or so.

When your wine has been racked a few times and shows NO more fermenting activity for a month or so (no bubbles in the airlock, no more sediment being produced), you can move on to bottling.

Follow the instructions on your selected type of wine stabilizer to stop fermentation. For potassium sorbate, this needs to be done 2-3 days before bottling.

Using sanitized equipment, take a final gravity reading, then rack the wine into clean, sanitized bottles. Cork, and store in a cool, dry place until use.

We like to use "Zorks" for corking our homemade wine. Easy to use – no special equipment needed! – easy to uncork, and – should you have any wine left in your bottle after serving - the "cork" is easily replaced for temporary storage

Maple Syrup Wine
168

Maple Syrup Wine

A funny thing happens when a couple of nerds take up home brewing... you start to look at things and think "Can I ferment that?" and "I wonder if...?". When one of those nerds happens to be Canadian, and you have a friend that works on a maple sugar farm... you end up with maple wine.

This wine isn't really wine - there's no fruit juice of any kind, never mind grape juice specifically - and it's not really mead, as there's no honey. I suppose it's closer to a mead than a wine, but it's a rare enough thing that I can't find proper terminology for it. It's actually easier to define it by what it isn't, than what it is!   Technical terminology aside, it IS delicious and unique!

The first time we made this, it was from maple sap that had only been boiled down part way - not full maple syrup.   As this is not a common ingredient, I've redeveloped the recipe to be more accessible.   As maple syrup is an expensive ingredient, I've scaled this down so you can try it in a small batch - feel free to multiply the ingredients to make a larger batch.

Using the Sweet Mead Yeast for this controls the degree to which it will ferment down, leaving a nice, sweet dessert wine. Feel free to play around with different types of yeast, to suit your wine preferences.

Makes slightly less than 1 gallon

Pure maple syrup	6 cups	1 ½ L
Bottled spring water	10 cups	2 ½ L
Acid blend	1/4 tsp	1 ml
Yeast nutrient	1 tsp	5 ml
White Labs Sweet Mead Yeast (WLP720)	1 vial	1 vial
Wine stabilizer of choice		

Equipment needed:

2 gallon pot
Two 1 gallon glass carboys & stoppers
1 air lock
Hydrometer, optional
Siphon, siphon tubing

Combine maple syrup and about half of the water in a large pot, stir until well combined. Add remaining water, stir once again to combine. Heat to ALMOST boiling – stirring constantly – then turn heat down and simmer gently for 10 minutes. Remove from heat, stir in acid blend and yeast nutrient.

Using a freshly sanitized ladle and funnel, transfer hot mixture into a freshly sanitized 1 gallon glass carboy. Cover with sanitized stopper and air lock, allow to cool to room temperature (overnight).

The next morning, take a gravity reading. Keep track of the number! (This is an optional step, but will allow you to calculate your final ABV % - See "Resources", page 229)

Sprinkle yeast into carboy, cover with sanitized cover and air lock, and gently swirl. Within 48 hours, you should notice fermentation activity – bubbles in the airlock, carbonation and /or swirling in the wine must. This means you're good to go!

Leave the carboy in a cool dark place to do its thing for a month or so.

Using sanitized equipment, rack the maple wine off the sediment, into a second clean, freshly sanitized gallon carboy. Cap with sanitized airlock, leave it alone for another 2-3 months.

Rack one more time, leave it for another 3 months or so.

When your wine has been racked a few times and shows NO more fermenting activity for a month or so (no bubbles in the airlock, no more sediment being produced), you can move on to bottling.

Follow the instructions on your selected type of wine stabilizer to stop fermentation. For potassium sorbate, this needs to be done 2-3 days before bottling.

Using sanitized equipment, take a final gravity reading, then rack the wine into clean, sanitized bottles. Cork, and store in a cool, dry place until use.

We like to use "Zorks" for corking our homemade wine. Easy to use – no special equipment needed! – easy to uncork, and – should you have any wine left in your bottle after serving, the "cork" is easily replaced for temporary storage

Bloody Caesar

The Caesar (or "Bloody Caesar") is the one of - if not THE - most popular mixed drinks in Canada. It was first created in the late 60s, by a Calgary restaurant manager. In the initial incarnation, whole ingredients - tomato juice, clams, etc - were brought together to create the signature drink. Later on, the Mott's company came out with Clamato ® cocktail mix, which made things easier for everyone.

Like its cousin the Bloody Mary, Caesars are very customizable. While unflavoured, high quality vodka is the standard, feel free to play with savoury flavoured ones - cucumber vodka, pepper flavoured vodkas, horseradish infused vodka, etc all work beautifully. Additionally, you can have just as much fun with the garnishes as you do with Bloody Marys. A celery spear, slice of lime, and stick of olives is pretty traditional... but there are restaurants that garnish the drink with entire meals - sandwiches, burgers, onion rings, a whole roasted chicken, etc.

I'll be honest - I didn't try a Caesar until I learned to make them at the Toronto Institute of Bartending, as Clamato sounded pretty gross to me before then. I would imagine the "Clamato sounds gross" thing - as well as the sketchy availability of Clamato in many areas - contributes to Caesars lack of popularity outside of Canada / areas with a lot of Canadians. If you can find Clamato where you are, use it for the cocktail mix. If not, see my recipe for tomato-clam cocktail mix, on page 172.

Anyway... I've since learned the error of my thinking, though I still prefer fruity tropical drinks. This tastes like home, though... and rum drinks don't.

Per glass:

Lime wedge	1	1
Celery Salt		
Coarse ground black pepper (optional)		
Celery stalk	1	1
Vodka of choice	1 - 1 ½ oz	1 - 1 ½ oz
Tabasco sauce	2 dashes	2 dashes
Salt	3 dashes	3 dashes
Pepper	3 dashes	3 dashes
Worcestershire sauce	4 dashes	4 dashes
Tomato-clam cocktail mix		

Use the lime wedge to wet the rim of a tall glass, and invert it onto a plate of celery salt. (I like to mix a little coarse ground pepper into the celery salt, but that's entirely optional.)

Fill glass to just above the rim with ice, place celery stalk in class.

Pour vodka over ice, followed by Tabasco sauce, salt, pepper, and Worcestershire sauce. Fill glass with tomato clam cocktail mix, stopping just below the celery salt rim. Garnish as desired, serve immediately.

Tomato-Clam Cocktail Mix

Tomato juice	1 ½ cups	375 ml
Clam juice	1 cup	250 ml
Granulated sugar	5 tsp	25 ml
White vinegar	2-3 tsp	10-15 ml
Onion powder	1/4 tsp	1 ml
Garlic powder	1/8 tsp	½ ml
Ground black pepper	pinch	pinch
Cayenne	pinch	pinch
Celery seed	pinch	pinch

Whisk everything together, taste. Adjust seasonings for personal taste.

Bloody Caesar

Confetti Bars

Desserts

Confetti Bars

Back home in Winnipeg, you can't go to a potluck, holiday dinner, or wedding social without coming across these things. They're the kind of thing you learn to make as a youngster, and pretty much everyone - in the areas where they're popular, anyway - just knows how to make.

... and they're highly addictive. When I realized that they weren't a common thing in the USA, I wondered if my friends would like it, or if it was one of those things where the deliciousness of it is half nostalgia. Given how fast they disappear... I'd say generally addictive!

While rainbow marshmallows are traditional, these are also commonly made with plain / white mini marshmallows. I heartily encourage starting with the rainbow ones, if you can find them!

This is a super simple recipe, and it takes only about 5 minutes to make.

Makes 1 pan of bars

Butter or pan spray		
Butter	½ cup	125 ml
Creamy peanut butter	1 cup	250 ml
1 package butterscotch chips	11 oz	311 g
Rainbow coloured mini marshmallows	~10 oz	283 g

Generously grease a pan - 8"x 8" yields thicker bars, as pictured, while 9" x 13" yields more, thin bars. Set aside.

In a glass bowl, heat butter, peanut butter, and butterscotch chips. I like to microwave it for a minute or so, until the chips are about half melted. Stir until everything is melted, combined, and smooth. Allow to cool slightly, without solidifying.

Add in mini marshmallows, stir until all are evenly coated. Use between ½ and 1 bag of them, depending on your tastes. I usually use about 2/3 of a bag, but used a whole bag for this batch (as pictured). Sometimes you want more of the "fudge" part, sometimes you want more marshmallows. These bars are NOT a hard science!

When marshmallows are coated, spread mixture into prepared pan. Chill until set, use a sharp knife to cut into bars.

Puffed Wheat Squares

Puffed Wheat Squares

Much like the confetti bar, this is a super popular bar back home in Winnipeg, and it seems to be mostly a Canadian Prairies thing.

You know how you can get Crispy Rice squares pretty much anywhere, even in the gas stations? It's the same way with these bars back home.

These are super quick and easy to make, and are definitely "comfort" food. Even just that earthy, roasty aroma of the puffed wheat, any time I make these and just open the bag of cereal... Mmm. Memories!

Note: A 6 oz bag of cereal works out to be about 11 cups.

Makes a 9" x 13" pan of squares

Puffed wheat cereal	6 oz	170 g
Butter	½ cup	125 ml
Brown sugar packed	1 cup	250 ml
Corn syrup	1 cup	250 ml
Cocoa powder	2/3 cup	150 ml
Salt	½ tsp	2 ml
Vanilla extract	1 tsp	5 ml

Generously grease a 9" x 13" baking pan, set aside. Pour puffed wheat into a large, heat-proof mixing bowl.

In a medium saucepan, combine butter, brown sugar, corn syrup, cocoa, and salt. Heat over medium until butter melts.

Once butter melts, turn heat up a bit and bring mixture to a boil. Boil for 2 minutes, then remove from heat and stir in vanilla until well combined.

Pour hot chocolate mixture over puffed wheat, stir (carefully!) until all of the wheat is coated with chocolate. Pour mixture into prepared baking pan.

Using lightly greased (or slightly damp!) hands, firmly press mixture down into the pan, until compacted and relatively flat. Allow to cool and set completely before cutting into squares.

For Gluten-free: Use gluten-free puffed rice cereal in place of the puffed wheat cereal. Make sure it's the soft kind, not crisp.

Matrimonial Cake

These oat and date squares are very popular across most of Canada, but especially in prairies (They're called "date squares" outside of the prairies). Ubiquitous at potlucks and on holiday dessert trays, these are pretty simple to make... and very satisfying! My husband and I like to convince ourselves that these qualify has a healthy breakfast food... hah!

Makes a 9"x13" pan of bars

Pitted dates, chopped	1 lb	500 g
Water	1 ½ cups	375 ml
Brown sugar, packed	½ cup	125 ml
Rolled oats	3 cups	750 ml
All-purpose flour	2 ½ cups	625 ml
Brown sugar, packed	1 ½ cups	375 ml
Baking soda	2 tsp	10 ml
Salt	½ tsp	2 ml
Butter, softened	1 3/4 cup	425 ml

Preheat oven to 350 F (180 C), grease a 9" x 13" pan, set aside

In a medium saucepan, combine dates, water, and brown sugar. Bring just to a boil, then reduce heat and simmer for 7-10 minutes, until thick.

As filling is simmering, combine oats, flour, brown sugar, baking soda, and salt in a large bowl. Mix well. You can use a wooden spoon, potato masher, or - clean! - hands to blend the butter into the dry mix. You want to get the butter mixed in well, forming a crumbly mixture.

Spread half of the oat mixture into the pan. Press down firmly and evenly to form a crust. Once date mixture is ready, spread on top of oat crust. Scatter date mixture evenly with remaining oat mixture. Use clean hands to press down gently and evenly on topping to compress everything together.

Bake for 35-40 minutes, until top is golden brown. Remove from oven, allow to cool to room temperature. Use a sharp knife to cut into squares.

For Gluten-free: Omit all-purpose flour. Mix together 1 cup light buckwheat flour, 1 cup sorghum flour, 1/4 cup coconut flour, and 3/4 tsp xanthan gum, use in place of all-purpose flour. Be sure to use gluten-free certified oats and oat flour. Increase butter to 2 cups.

Matrimonial Cake

Nanaimo Bars

Picture it. Vancouver, Canada... 1986. I was a little girl on the trip of a lifetime – experiencing Expo '86. I was young enough that most of the memories from it are now a blur, or reduced to general feelings and thoughts ("That was cool!"), but 2 few things stood out then, and still remain fresh in my mind today: The Ramses II exhibit, and very first Nanaimo Bar. The Ramses II exhibit was easily the coolest part of Expo 86, and the bar was a bite of heaven; a sugar rush that no sane parent should ever get their kids jacked up on!

The Nanaimo Bar is a Canadian specialty – named after a town in British Columbia – and it's very hard to find anything like them outside of Canada. As with many things though.. if you can't buy them.. you can always make them! This recipe is for basic, "original" flavoured Nanaimo bars - a classic. The middle layer can be flavoured any number of ways, using whatever extracts or flavourings you like, though! Gluten-Free graham crumbs can be substituted, but instant pudding powder CANNOT be substituted with anything but "custard powder", which is traditional but hard to come by.

Makes an 8"x8" pan of bars

Unsalted butter	½ cup	125 ml
Granulated sugar	1/4 cup	50 ml
Cocoa powder	6 Tbsp	90 ml
Large egg, beaten	1	1
Graham cracker crumbs	1 1/4 cup	300 ml
Sliced almonds, finely chopped	½ cup	125 ml
Unsweetened coconut flakes	1 cup	250 ml
Unsalted butter	½ cup	125 ml
Heavy whipping cream	3 Tbsp	45 ml
Cook & Serve vanilla pudding powder	3 Tbsp	45 ml
Icing (powdered/confectioner) sugar	2 cups+	500 ml +
Semi sweet baking chocolate squares	6 oz	170 g
Butter	3 Tbsp	45 ml

Melt butter in small saucepan. Add sugar and cocoa powder, mix well. Add egg, stir well. Egg will cook and thicken. Once mixture has thickened, remove from heat and pour into a larger bowl containing crumbs, almonds, and coconut flakes. Mix well and press firmly and evenly into the bottom of an ungreased 8 x 8 pan. Set aside.

Cream butter and heavy cream. Add pudding powder, beat well. Slowly and carefully add powdered sugar. Mixture should be VERY thick – add a little extra powdered sugar if needed. Spread evenly over bottom layer.

Melt butter and chocolate over low heat. Remove from heat, allow to cool slightly, then pour and spread over middle layer. Chill in fridge before slicing into bars

Nanaimo Bars

Sucre à la Crème

This is a traditional Quebec fudge recipe, contributed by my friend Karine Charlebois.

This was how her grandmother made it - the recipe was passed down to her mother, down to Karine, and finally on to you! Big thanks to Karine for her patience as I used my very rusty grasp on French to translate the original as best I could, before bugging her for help.

Also, a note on preparing the pan: "also for authenticity, the pan should be buttered instead of sprayed, but it all works in the end. As long as you use a stickiness prevention method!"

Makes an 8" x 8" pan of fudge

Heavy whipping cream	1 cup	250 ml
Dark brown sugar, packed	2 cups	500 ml
Butter	1 Tbsp	15 ml

Prepare an 8x8"pan: Butter, spray with nonstick spray, or and/or line with parchment paper, set aside.

In a large saucepan, combine cream and brown sugar. Affix a candy thermometer to the pan; bring mixture to a boil over medium heat, stirring constantly.

When mixture reaches 240 F (115 C) - soft ball stage - remove from heat and stir in butter. Carefully beat the sugar mixture until it loses its shine - you'll see it start to crust on the sides of the saucepan.

Pour into prepared pan, allow to cool for 5-10 minutes before cutting. Allow to cool completely before removing from pan.

Variations:

Maple or Vanilla: Add about 1 tsp (5 ml) of extract before the butter.

Coffee: Dissolve 1-2 tsp (5-10 ml) instant coffee granules in hot cream, before adding the brown sugar.

Peanut Butter: Omit the butter. Add 1 cup (250 ml) of creamy peanut butter once you remove the sugar from the heat, beat as normal.

Coffee & Vanilla Sucre à la Crème

Butter Tart Bars

Butter tart bars are a quick and easy way to to indulge that "I would shank someone for a butter tart" urge that many of us Canadians Abroad tend to get, requiring far less effort than making actual Butter Tarts (Page 193).

These are always a huge hit anywhere I bring them - original or gluten-free version, shared with Americans and Canadians alike!

Makes an 8 x 8 pan of bars

All-purpose flour	1 1/3 cup	325 ml
Granulated sugar	1/4 cup	50 ml
Butter	½ cup	125 ml
Large egg	1	1
Brown sugar, packed	1 cup	250 ml
Corn starch	1 Tbsp	5 ml
All-purpose flour	1 Tbsp	5 ml
Baking powder	½ tsp	2 ml
Salt	1/4 tsp	1 ml
Butter, melted	1/4 cup	50 ml
Large eggs, beaten	3	3
Maple syrup	2 Tbsp	30 ml
Vanilla extract	1 tsp	5 ml
Dark raisins	1 cup	250 ml
Chopped walnuts, optional	½ cup	125 ml

Preheat oven to 350 F (180 C), Line 8x8" pan with parchment paper

Combine flour and sugar in a food processor. Add butter and egg, blitz until finely crumbly. Spread mixture out in prepared pan, distributing evenly. Firmly press to create a level crust. Bake for 15 minutes.

In a medium mixing bowl, whisk together brown sugar, corn starch, flour, baking powder and salt. Add butter, eggs, maple syrup and vanilla, whisk to combine well. Add raisins and walnuts (if using), stir. Pour mixture over crust. Bake bars for 20 minutes, remove from heat, cool to room temperature. Once cool, transfer to fridge and chill for an hour before cutting into squares.

Recipe can be doubled - Use a 9x13" pan. Do initial bake for 20 minutes, and second bake for 25-30 minutes

For Gluten-free: Omit all-purpose flour. Use a mixture of 2/3 cup sorghum flour, 1/3 cup sweet rice flour, 1/4 cup corn starch, and ½ tsp xanthan gum in dough, and 1 Tbsp sorghum in filling mixture

Butter Tart Bars

Imperial Cookies

A traditional sandwich cookie in Winnipeg - you can buy them anywhere, there! While raspberry jam is traditional, sometimes I like to mix it up a bit and use blackcurrant jam instead. Makes 25 3" sandwich cookies

Butter, softened	3/4 cup	175 ml
Granulated sugar	1 cup	250 ml
Large eggs	2	2
Large egg white	1	1
Vanilla extract	1 tsp	5 ml
Baking powder	1 tsp	5 ml
Salt	½ tsp	2 ml
All purpose flour	2 ½ cups	625 ml
Raspberry jam	½ cup +	125 ml+
Icing (powdered/confectioner) sugar	2 ½ cups	625 ml
Salt	pinch	pinch
Almond extract	1/4 tsp	1 ml
Hot water	2-3 Tbsp	30-45 ml

Red food colouring, gel icing, or finally chopped candied cherries

In a stand mixer, cream together butter and sugar until smooth and fluffy. Add in eggs and egg white, a little at a time, beating well between each addition. Add vanilla extract, and mix until well incorporated and smooth. Mix baking powder, salt, and flour together, carefully mix into wet ingredients until fully incorporated. Wrap dough in plastic film, chill for 1 hour.

Preheat oven to 400 F (200 C), line baking sheets with parchment paper. On a floured counter, roll cookie dough out to about 1/4" thick (can be slightly thicker). Use cookie cutters to cut out 3" scalloped rounds, place cookies 2" apart on prepared baking sheets. Bake cookies for 8-10 minutes, or until bottoms look lightly golden. Allow cookies to cool on baking sheets for at least 5 minutes before moving. Cookies need to cool completely before sandwiching.

While waiting for the cookies to cool, make your glaze: Use a fork to whisk together icing sugar and salt. Add almond extract and enough hot water to make a thin glaze.

Flip half of the cookies over, spread underside with jam. Top each with one of the remaining cookies. Spread top of each cookie sandwich with glaze, place a dot of red frosting (dyed remaining glaze), gel icing, or a piece of cherry while glaze is still wet. Allow cookies to sit, undisturbed, until set.

For Gluten-free: Omit all-purpose flour. Add a mixture of 1 cup brown rice flour, 1 cup sorghum flour, 1/4 cup coconut flour, 2 Tbsp tapioca starch, 2 tsp xanthan gum to the dry ingredients. Use corn starch for rolling

Imperial Cookies

Oatmeal Peanut Butter Sandwich Cookies

These cookies began as a craving for an off-the-shelf cookie from back home. My husband had never tried them, so I made a home version... and I was promptly informed that they were very much like a Girl Scout cookie he liked. Either way, these are a great cookie, and disappear FAST Makes about 30 2" sandwich cookies

Rolled Oats, chopped in food processor	½ cup	125 ml
Oat flour	3/4 cup	175 ml
All purpose flour	½ cup	125 ml
Baking powder	½ tsp	2 ml
Salt	½ tsp	2 ml
Smooth peanut butter	1/3 cup	75 ml
Granulated sugar	2/3 cup	150 ml
Large egg	1	1
Vanilla extract	1 tsp	5 ml
Peanut butter	1/3 cup	75 ml
Vanilla extract	½ tsp	2 ml
Salt	pinch	pinch
Icing (Powdered) sugar	2 cups	500 ml
Water	2 Tbsp	30 ml

Whisk together dry ingredients (except sugar) until well combined, set aside. In a stand mixer, cream together peanut butter and sugar until smooth and fluffy. Add in egg, beat well. Add vanilla extract, and mix until well incorporated and smooth. Slowly add dry mix to the mixer bowl, and carefully mix until well incorporated and smooth. Wrap dough in plastic film, chill for 1 hour.

Preheat oven to 350 F (180 C), line baking sheets with parchment paper. Generously sprinkle clean work surface with flour, roll dough to 1/8" thick. Use cookie cutters to cut out rounds, place cookies 1" apart on greased baking sheets. For authenticity, use a straw to poke a hole in the middle of half of the cookies. Bake cookies for 8-10 minutes, or until bottoms look lightly golden. Allow cookies to cool on baking sheets for at least 5 minutes before moving. Cookies need to cool completely before filling.

Whip peanut butter, vanilla extract and salt, until smooth and well incorporated. Slowly add powdered sugar a bit at a time, until incorporated completely. Beat on high for 1 minute – mixture will be very, very thick. Lower mixer speed to lowest setting, and slowly add water. Once incorporated, check for consistency. Add more water or powdered sugar to achieve the consistency you want. Spoon prepared filling into a pastry bag. Cut the tip off and pipe about a small amount of filling onto the bottom of one cookie. Flip over, top with another cookie, repeat with remaining cookies and filling.

Gluten-Free: Omit all-purpose flour. Add 3/4 cup gluten-free oat flour, 1/4 cup sorghum flour, 1/4 cup coconut flour, and 1 tsp xanthan gum in the dry mix. Use corn starch for rolling, and certified gf oats /oat flour.

Oatmeal Peanut Butter Sandwich Cookies

Pets De Soeurs

These are a traditional Quebec pastry / cookie... loosely translated as "Nun's Farts"!

Like many traditional foods, this is something that tends to be somewhat of a non-recipe. You roll out some pie dough, make a flavourful cinnamon paste - usually thrown together from memory / by feel - and go from there.

You can use whatever pie dough recipe you like, or buy pre-made. The Pate Brisee recipe for Butter Tarts (page 193) works well for this.

Makes 18-25 ish cookies

Two-crust batch of pastry dough	1	1
Brown sugar, packed	2/3 cup	150 ml
Butter, melted	1Tbsp	15 ml
Maple syrup	1 Tbsp	15 ml
Ground cinnamon	1/4 tsp	1 ml

Preheat oven to 375 F (190 C). Line two baking sheets with parchment paper.

Roll dough into rectangle, approximately 12x14".

Whisk together remaining ingredients, forming a thick, crumbly paste. Gently sprinkle / spread paste over top of rolled dough, leaving a 1" border with no paste.

Starting with one of the long sides of the rectangle, roll into a tight log, ending at the other long end. Pinch the seam side to seal.

Slice into rounds, about ½" thick. Transfer rounds to prepared baking sheets, leaving at least 1" between each. If ends come undone, pinch or tuck under to secure.

Bake for 12-15 minutes, or until golden brown.

For Gluten-Free:　Use a gluten-free pastry dough recipe. I have one on page 194.

Pets De Soeurs

Butter Tarts

Butter Tarts

For many non-Canadians, their only exposure to this national delicacy has been as a lyric in Len's "Steal my Sunshine" (in the radio version, anyway). They've been around forever, and you can get them anywhere in Canada… Tim Hortons.. gas stations.. even boxes of factory made ones, in among the snack cakes section.

Because butter tarts have been around forever, there are about a million versions of then. Some use brown sugar, some use white… most use corn syrup, I use maple syrup… you get the idea. If you like your butter tarts to be a little runny, only use 2 eggs in the filling. This makes 12-18 tarts, depending on shell size

Pre made tart shells or 1 batch pastry crust (recipe follows)		
Raisins	½ - 1 cup	125-250 ml
Unsalted butter, softened	1/3 cup	75 ml
Light brown sugar, packed	1 cup	250 ml
Maple syrup	1/4 cup	50 ml
Large eggs, whisked	3	3

Preheat oven to 375 F (190 C)

Prepare pastry crust recipe, if using. If using pre made pie crust, roll cut out and prepare tart shells per directions in the tart shells recipe below. Divide raisins among tart shells – I personally like to have a fair amount of raisins in my butter tarts, so I use 1 cup. (½ cup is probably closer to average!). Set aside.

Combine butter, brown sugar, and maple syrup in a medium saucepan. Beat until smooth. Add in eggs, beat once more until well combined. Heat mixture on medium, stirring constantly. Bring mixture JUST to a boil, remove from heat. Carefully pour mixture into prepared tart shells.

Bake for 15-20 minutes, until filling has set and the pastry is lightly browned. Remove from oven and allow to cool. These are usually served at room temperature, but some prefer them chilled!

For Gluten-Free: Use Gluten-Free Pastry Crust recipe, page 194.

Pastry Crust (Pate Brisee)

All-purpose flour	1 1/4 cups	300 ml
Salt	½ tsp	2 ml
Granulated sugar	1 Tbsp	15 ml
Unsalted butter, chilled	½ cup	125 ml
Ice water	1/8 to 1/4 cup	25-50 ml

Combine flour, salt, and sugar in a food processor. Chop chilled butter into small cubes, add to flour mixture, and process 15-20 seconds, until it resembles fine gravel.

While running processor, stream 1/8 cup of ice water into the flour mixture, just until dough holds together when pinched. If necessary, add more water.

Dump dough out onto a work surface, gather into a disk shape. Wrap with plastic wrap, chill for 1 hour.

Lightly flour your work surface, roll chilled dough out pretty thin – 1/8" to 1/4", depending on your tastes – some prefer a thinner shell, some thicker. Cut 4" rounds from the pastry – you're aiming for 12.

Carefully transfer the pastry rounds to a muffin pan. I like to flatten the bottom against the tin, and work out from there, flattening the whole round to be flush with the muffin pan cavity – it holds the most filling! Feel free to get decorative about it – flattening the bottom of the dough against the muffin pan, gently ruffling the edges… it's up to you! Chill the pan of prepared tart shells until ready to use.

Gluten-free Pastry Crust

Makes enough for 18 or more tart shells - make Pets de Soeurs with remaining dough, or increase filling recipe by 50%

White rice flour	3/4 cup	175 ml
Light buckwheat flour	3/4 cup	175 ml
Millet flour	½ cup	125 ml
Sweet rice flour	1/4 cup	50 ml
Corn starch, plus extra for rolling	1/4 cup	50 ml
Granulated sugar	2 Tbsp	30 ml
Xanthan gum	2 tsp	10 ml
Brick cream cheese	8oz	250 g
Cold butter	½ cup	125 ml
Large egg	1	1
Cold water	1/4 cup	50 ml

Measure flours, corn starch, sugar and xanthan gum into the bowl of your food processor, blitz to combine. Add cream cheese, butter, and egg, blitz a few times until mixture resembles gravel. Stream in cold water as you run the food processor, just long enough to bring it together as a dough.

Remove dough from processor, knead lightly to bring it together as a ball. Wrap in plastic film, chill for 1 hour. Use additional corn starch for rolling.

Cape Breton Pork Pies

Pork pies in the dessert chapter? Yes... there's no actual pork involved here! These are adorable little tarts: cookie shell, sweet date filling, with a maple syrup frosting dollop on top.

As the name implies, this dessert hails from Nova Scotia, where they are most commonly seen around the holidays.

I like to do these up as mini, "2 bite" type tarts, as they're usually part of a large dainties spread. If you're not keeping "sample everything!" needs in mind, you can do these up as about 24 normal sized tarts, using regular sized muffin tins.

Makes about 48 mini tarts

Butter	1 cup	250 ml
Icing (powdered/confectioner) sugar	1/3 cup	75 ml
Large egg	1	1
Milk	1 Tbsp	15 ml
Vanilla extract	½ tsp	2 ml
All-purpose flour	2 1/4 cups	550 ml
Salt	pinch	pinch
Pitted Dates	1 lb	500 g
Water	1 cup	250 ml
Brown Sugar, packed	¾ cup	175 ml
Orange, zest of	1	1
Salt	pinch	pinch
Vanilla extract	1 tsp	5 ml
Butter, softened	2 Tbsp	30 ml
Maple syrup	2 Tbsp	30 ml
Icing (powdered/confectioner) sugar	1 ½ cups	375 ml
Milk	1 tsp	5 ml

Preheat oven to 325 F (160 C). Spray two mini cupcake pans with pan spray, set aside.

In a stand mixer, cream together butter and powdered sugar until smooth and fluffy. Add in egg, milk, and vanilla extract; mix until well incorporated and smooth.

Mix flour and salt together, carefully mix into wet ingredients until fully incorporated.

Divide dough into 48 equal sized balls. Using clean hands, flatten each ball into a disk, place into a mini muffin pan cavity, and press into the bottom / up the sides, forming a tart shell. Repeat with remaining dough balls.

195

Bake for about 15 minutes, until lightly golden brown. Set aside to cool.

Finely chop pitted dates, add to a medium saucepan along with water, brown sugar, orange zest, and salt. Bring to a boil, reduce heat and simmer gently for 5 minutes, stirring and mashing the dates frequently.

Once thickened, remove from heat, stir in vanilla, and let rest for 10 minutes. Spoon into baked shells.

Whip butter and maple syrup together until smooth. Slowly add powdered sugar a bit at a time, until incorporated completely. Beat on high for 1 minute – mixture will be very, very thick.

Lower mixer speed to lowest setting, and slowly add milk. Once incorporated, check for consistency - you want it thick, but soft enough to pipe. Add more milk or sugar to achieve the consistency you want.

Spoon or pipe small dollops of frosting on top of each tart.

For Gluten-free: Omit all-purpose flour in the crust dough. Mix together 1 cup light buckwheat flour, ½ cup white rice flour, 1/4 cup sweet rice flour, 1/4 cup corn starch, and ½ tsp xanthan gum (optional), add as dry mixture, in place of the flour. Use corn starch for rolling.

Cape Breton Pork Pies

Flapper Pie

Flapper Pie is one of those things whose origins REALLY depend on who you ask. It might be from Winnipeg, it might be from Saskatchewan... and some places in Alberta claim it as their own. Either way, it's definitely a prairie thing. This is not an elegant food. Crumb crust plus custard = not a lot of structural integrity. Add in the fussiness of meringue, and this is definitely something you'll want to eat the same day you make it. That shouldn't be a difficult thing to manage, though - super comfort food, right here.

Makes 1 pie

Graham cracker crumbs	1 1/4 cups	300 ml
Granulated sugar	1/3 cup	75 ml
Cinnamon	1/4 tsp	1 ml
Butter, melted	1/4 cup	50 ml
Large egg whites	4	4
Granulated sugar	1/3 cup	75 ml
Cream of tartar	1/4 tsp	1 ml
Salt	pinch	pinch
Granulated sugar	1/3 cup	75 ml
Cornstarch	1/4 cup	50 ml
Large egg yolks, lightly beaten	4	4
Milk	2 ½ cups	625 ml
Vanilla extract	1 tsp	5 ml

Preheat oven to 350 F (180 C). Combine graham crumbs, sugar, and cinnamon. Add melted butter, mix completely incorporated & moistened. Evenly distribute across the bottom and sides of a 9" pie plate, reserving 2 Tbsp for topping. Press ingredients firmly, extending crust partway up the sides of the pan. Bake for 12 minutes, remove from heat, allow to cool.

In a stand mixer - or a large bowl with a hand mixer - combine egg whites, sugar, cream of tartar, and salt. Beat egg white mixture until stiff peaks form. As egg whites are beating, whisk together sugar, cornstarch, and egg yolks in a medium saucepan, until smooth and well combined. Add in milk, a little at a time, whisking again until smooth and well incorporated. Cook custard mixture over medium-high heat until it boils. Turn heat down to medium low, and whisk constantly until mixture thickens. Remove from heat, whisk in vanilla extract.

Spoon hot custard mixture into cooled, pre-baked pie shell. Immediately spread meringue over pie filling, completely covering all exposed filling. Sprinkle reserved crumb mixture over top. Bake for 15 minutes, or until edges of meringue are golden. Cool to room temperature before refrigerating - UNCOVERED - for 2-3 hours before serving.

For Gluten-free: Use gluten-free graham cracker crumbs.

Flapper Pie

Tarte Au Sucre

AKA "Sugar Pie", this is a traditional Quebec dessert. As with the Sucre à la Crème (page 182), this recipe comes from my friend Karine Charlebois.

The use of flour in the filling isn't super traditional. Karine's mom says that it "just serves to make the contents not runny and more fluffy"

Makes 1 pie

Unbaked pie crust	1	1
1 can evaporated milk	12oz	354 ml
All-purpose flour	4 Tbsp	60 ml
Dark brown sugar, packed	2 cups	500 ml
Large eggs	2	2
Vanilla extract	1 tsp	5 ml
Butter, melted	2 Tbsp	30 ml

Preheat oven to 375 F (190 C).

Whisk together all ingredients, pour into pie crust.

Bake pie for 40-45 minutes, or until almost set. Remove from oven.

Allow to cool before cutting and serving.

Maple Syrup Variation: Decrease brown sugar to 1 cup, add 1 cup of maple syrup. Add 1 extra egg to the mix.

For Gluten-free: Use a gluten-free pie crust recipe, and 1/3 cup light buckwheat OR sorghum flour in the batter.

Tarte Au Sucre

Schmoo Torte

Schmoo Torte

Schmoo torte is very much a Winnipeg thing, though locals don't tend to *know* how exclusively Winnipeg it is, til they move away!

Schmoo - or "Shmoo", depending on who's writing it - is a soft, pecan-laced angel food cake that is torted and filled with sweetened whipped cream, before being served up with a buttery caramel sauce.

This decadent cake is served at various bakeries and dessert restaurants around the city, and apparently it's very common at Winnipeg Bar Mitzvahs- but you don't really see it anywhere else.

While it's not generally something that people tend to make at home, it's not actually all that difficult to make.

Serves about 8-12

Large egg whites	12	12
Cake flour	1 cup	250 ml
Pecan meal / flour	1 cup	250 ml
Baking powder	1 tsp	5 ml
Cream of tartar	1 tsp	5 ml
Salt	pinch	pinch
Granulated sugar	1 1/3 cup	325 ml
Vanilla extract	1 tsp	5 ml
Heavy whipping cream	2 cups	500 ml
Icing (Powdered) sugar	3 Tbsp	45 ml
Vanilla extract	1 tsp	5 ml
Butter	½ cup	125 ml
Brown sugar, packed	1 ½ cups	375 ml
Heavy cream	½ cup	125 ml
Vanilla extract	1 tsp	5 ml

Preheat oven to 350 F (180 C). Line the bottom of a 10" tube / angel food cake pan with parchment paper, set aside. (Do not grease the pan)

Separate egg whites into the bowl of a stand mixer, allow to stand at room temperature for about 20 minutes. In a separate bowl, mix together the flour, pecan meal, and baking powder; set aside.

Add cream of tartar and salt to the egg whites, use a whisk attachment to bear on low until combined. Turn speed up to high, beat until stiff peaks form. Turn speed down to medium, and slowly add the sugar, a little at a time, until combined. Turn speed to low, add vanilla, mix just until combined.

Remove bowl from stand mixer, gently fold in the flour mixture - about ½ cup at a time - JUST until combined.

Gently spoon mixture into tube pan. Bake for 35-40 minutes, or until a knife inserted into the middle of the cake comes out clean.

Invert cake onto a cooling rack - leaving it in the pan - and allow to cool for about an hour. Remove pan, slice cake into 3 equally thick layers.

Whisk 2 cups of the heavy whipping cream together with the icing sugar and vanilla until very thick. Spread as filling between the 3 cake layers, stacking as you go. Use remaining whipped cream to frost the sides and center of the cake, chill for at least two hours.

Melt butter in a medium saucepan. Add brown sugar and heavy cream, whisking until smooth. Bring to a boil over medium heat. Boil for 2 minutes - stirring constantly - then remove from heat. Stir in vanilla, allow to cool.

To serve, warm the sauce, drizzle over whole torte, and/or individual slices.

For Gluten-free: Mix together 1/3 cup light buckwheat flour, 1/4 cup corn starch, 1/4 cup coconut flour, 2 Tbsp tapioca starch, and ½ tsp xanthan gum, use in place of the cake flour.

Frozen Chocolate Cake

This is a weird one. I wrote a whole cookbook of fabulous cake recipes, was always known for making tasty cakes, and here I am trying to duplicate a ... well, not spectacular chocolate cake. Total comfort food, sure... but technically not a good cake. It was a *hugely* popular request from expats while developing this book, though.

The fun in this one came from trying to replicate a cake and frosting that doesn't really attain a "frozen" texture when frozen. It's actually kind of horrifying when you start really thinking about it, the crimes against cake that may have been committed to make the source material work! I promised to not include anything TOO weird, preferring to have frosting that does sort of freeze, than a complete Frankencake.

In the end, the cake required swapping oil in for butter (butter tastes better, but affects the frozen texture!), and the decision to use something other than frosting as the frosting. My "eureka" moment came as I was sorting through recipes to post to the blog, coming across my Earl Grey pie as a possibility. While it's a custard recipe, it made me think - it was originally going to be based on a French Silk pie. French Silk pie filling is remarkably close to the taste and texture of the not-frozen, frozen "frosting"... and here we are!

When making the "frosting", it's best to keep everything as cold as possible. If you can chill the bowl and whisk attachment for your stand mixer before making this, it works better. I like to put the eggs in the freezer for a few minutes before using, also. Be sure to use pasteurized eggs, as they are not cooked in this recipe!

Makes a 9 x 13" pan of cake

Cake flour	2 cups	500 ml
Cocoa powder	1/3 cup	75 ml
Sugar	1 ½ cups	375 ml
Baking powder	4 tsp	20 ml
Salt	1 tsp	5 ml
Instant vanilla pudding mix	3 ½ oz	96 g
Large eggs	4	4
Water	1 cup	250 ml
Vegetable Oil	½ cup	125 ml
Vanilla extract	1 tsp	5 ml
Unsweetened baking chocolate squares	4 oz	125 g
Butter, room temperature	1 cup	250 ml
Granulated sugar	1 1/4 cups	300 ml
Cocoa powder	1 Tbsp	15 ml
Vanilla extract	1 tsp	5 ml
Large pasteurized eggs	4	4
Chocolate Sprinkles, optional		

Preheat oven to 350 F (180 C). Liberally grease a 9 x 13" cake pan with vegetable shortening, and/or spray with baking spray.

Combine flour, cocoa powder, sugar, baking powder, salt, and pudding mix in a large mixing bowl. Add in eggs and water, beating until smooth. Carefully add vegetable oil and vanilla to the mix, mixing on medium speed until smooth.

Pour batter into prepared cake pan. Bake until golden and knife inserted into center of batter comes out clean and cake springs back - about 25-30 minutes. Allow to cool 10-15 minutes before turning cake out onto baking rack to cool fully. Ideally, allow to cool to room temperature, wrap tightly with plastic wrap. Allow cake to sit overnight, making frosting the following day:

Melt baking chocolate: I like to do so in a glass bowl in the microwave, but doing so on the stove top over low heat is another option. Either way, melt until smooth, remove from heat, and allow to cool to almost room temperature - but not solidifying.

In the meantime, beat together butter and sugar in a stand mixer - or with an electric mixer - until pale and fluffy. Add cocoa powder and vanilla, beat on low until blended. Add cooled chocolate, beat once more until completely blended in.

Take one egg from the fridge or freezer, crack it into the mix, and beat until mixed in. Turn speed up to medium-high, and beat for 4-5 minutes. Repeat with remaining eggs - 4-5 minutes apart. Leave eggs chilling while waiting to add them. Once final egg has been beaten for 4-5 minutes, cover bowl with plastic wrap, chill for at least one hour.

Spoon a small amount of frosting into a pastry bag fitted with a star attachment, pipe stars onto cooled cake. Refill bag with small amounts of frosting as you go - having too much in the bag at one time will have the frosting being warmed from your hands. If frosting is/becomes too runny to pipe, return to fridge to cool / firm up for a bit.

Once top of cake is covered in piped stars, scatter chocolate sprinkles on top (if desired), cover, and freeze.

Slice and serve straight out of the freezer, or allow slices to thaw slightly before serving.

For Gluten-Free: Mix together 1 1/4 cup light buckwheat flour, 1/4 cup sorghum flour, 1/4 cup coconut flour, and 3/4 tsp xanthan gum. Use in place of cake flour.

Frozen Chocolate Cake

Pouding Chômeur

This "Poor man's pudding" is a traditional dish from Quebec - more of a cake, than a pudding. It reminds me a lot of these instant dessert puddings we'd buy as a kid. You'd mix together batter ingredients in a pant, sprinkle the sauce/flavour powder over top, and finally add water. The "cake" part would cook up, leaving a bit of sauce on top, but most underneath. Very similar concept, here.

I like to use an 8.25" round casserole dish that is about 3" tall, but this also works in a 9x13" cake pan. Use whichever you have on hand, just decrease baking time slightly if using the 9 x 13" pan.

Crisco, lard, or butter for greasing

Butter	1/3 cup	75 ml
Granulated sugar	3/4 cup	175 ml
Milk	½ cup	125 ml
Large egg	1	1
Vanilla extract	1 tsp	5 ml
All-purpose flour	1 ½ cups	375 ml
Baking powder	1 ½ tsp	7 ml
Salt	1/4 tsp	1 ml
Maple syrup	1 cup	250 ml
Brown sugar, packed	1 cup	250 ml
Water	1 cup	250 ml
Butter	1/4 cup	50 ml

Preheat oven to 325 F (160 C). Grease a baking dish, set aside.

In a stand mixer, cream together butter and sugar until smooth and fluffy. Add in milk, egg, and vanilla extract; mix until well incorporated and smooth. Mix flour, baking powder, and salt together, carefully mix into wet ingredients until fully incorporated. Pour batter into prepared baking dish, set aside.

In a medium sized pot, combine maple syrup, brown sugar, water, and butter. Bring to a boil over medium heat. Turn down and allow mixture to simmer for 3 minutes.

Pour syrup over cake batter. Without stirring, transfer to preheated oven and bake for 40-45 minutes, or until cake is golden brown and a toothpick/knife inserted in the center comes out clean. Allow to cool slightly before serving. Serve warm, with or without whipped cream or ice cream

For Gluten-free: Add an extra egg. Mix together 3/4 cup Light buckwheat flour, 1/4 cup sweet rice flour, 1/4 cup coconut flour, and ½ tsp xanthan gum, use in place of the all-purpose flour.

Pouding Chômeur

Blueberry Grunt

Blueberry grunt is an old fashioned, traditional dessert from Nova Scotia - where wild blueberries are plentiful. A stove top type of cobbler, it features sweetened dumplings cooked in a mess of blueberries and sauce... and "grunt" comes from the sound of the blueberries cooking. Sometimes I'll make a spiced grunt, sometimes I leave the spices out. Sometimes I'll make it with lemon, as is traditional... but sometimes, I'll add in some grated orange peel. It's a very casual dessert, after all! Just be sure to not cook the berries down too far - you'll want a fair amount of sauce to steam the dumplings, and prevent the dish from burning.

Serves 4-6

Fresh blueberries	4 cups	1000 ml
Granulated sugar	3/4 cup	175 ml
Water	1 cup	250 ml
Lemon juice	2 tsp	10 ml
Cinnamon, optional	½ tsp	2 ml
Salt	1/4 tsp	1 ml
Ground nutmeg , optional	pinch	pinch
All-purpose flour	2 cups	500 ml
Granulated sugar	2 Tbsp	30 ml
Baking powder	1 Tbsp	15 ml
Salt	1 tsp	5 ml
Cold butter	1/4 cup	50 ml
Milk or buttermilk	1 cup	250 ml

In a medium-large, lidded pan or pot, combine blueberries, sugar, water, lemon juice, cinnamon, salt, and nutmeg. Bring to a boil, then reduce heat and simmer, while you make the batter:

In a medium sized bowl, mix together flour, sugar, baking powder, and salt. Measure butter into the same bowl, and cut into the dry ingredients using a pastry cutter or fork(s). The idea is to work it in until it's evenly distributed throughout, in very small pieces. Add milk/buttermilk, stir just until dough comes together. Don't over stir or beat it.

Keep an eye on your blueberries. Once the sauce has cooked down a bit and the blueberries have started to soften, drop rounded tablespoons worth of dough into simmering blueberries. Cover and simmer for 15 minutes WITHOUT LIFTING THE LID. Serve hot, with whipped cream or ice cream.

For gluten-free: Mix together 1 cup light buckwheat flour, 1/4 cup sorghum flour, 1/4 cup Potato starch, and 1/4 cup coconut flour, use in place of the all-purpose flour.

Blueberry Grunt

Persians

212

Persians

After my husband and I had made our big "buy all of the source material" trip home to Winnipeg, we got a request for Persian buns - a Thunder Bay thing.

I was told that this doughnut is HUGE there - in stores, at school cafeterias, as fundraisers, and with expats bringing cases of them after visiting home. It's basically a deep fried, slightly-flattened cinnamon roll, frosted with a signature frosting. Apparently there is a TON of debate about whether it's strawberries or raspberries in the frosting, and seen as a mystery.

Well, that's all I needed to hear - challenge accepted! We drove the 7ish hours each way - across the border - to buy a doughnut.

As it turns out, the original bakery also supplies Walmart, and as such... has their ingredients listed on each retail package. No mystery to tackle, after all - it was a combo of raspberry and apple. Oops.

A note on the frosting: If you want this to be authentic, you're going to need to use vegetable shortening in place of the butter; there is absolutely no butter in the real thing. I'm really not a fan of shortening-based frosting, though... so consider my recipe an upgrade! Other than that, I am staying true to the source material flavouring, which lists "apple raspberry jam" on the ingredients label. Feel free to play around with using fresh or frozen raspberries in place of the jam.

Makes 12 doughnuts

Warm - NOT hot! - water	1 ½ cups	375 ml
Active dry yeast	4 tsp	60 ml
Granulated sugar	3 Tbsp	45 ml
All-purpose flour	3 ½ cups	800 ml
Salt	1 tsp	5 ml
Butter, melted & cooled	1/4 cup	50 ml
Sugar	½ cup	125 ml
Ground cinnamon	1 Tbsp	15 ml
Butter, softened	1/4 cup	50 ml
Apple jelly	1/4 cup	50 ml
Seedless raspberry jam	1/4 cup	50 ml
Icing (powdered/confectioner) sugar	4+ cups	1000 ml+
Milk	2 Tbsp	30 ml

Stir yeast and sugar into warm water, allow to stand for 10 minutes – it should get very bubbly.

In a large mixing bowl, combine flour and salt. Pour in yeast mixture, stir well to combine. Dump dough out onto a floured surface, knead until soft and elastic, 5-10 minutes. (OR: mix it in a stand mixer with a dough hook for 5 minutes or so!)

Once dough is fully kneaded, place in a greased bowl, cover with plastic wrap, and allow to rise for one hour, or until doubled in size. Line a couple of baking sheets with parchment paper, set aside.

Once dough has doubled in size, roll dough out on a floured surface. Aim to make it a large rectangle, say 12 x 18" or so. Use a pastry brush to spread melted butter all over the dough – you might not use it all, that's ok. Mix together the sugar and cinnamon, sprinkle evenly over the melted butter.

Starting with one of the longer edges, tightly roll the dough up. Use a sharp knife to trim the ends so that they are flat, then slice the roll into 12 even rounds. Slightly flatten each roll between your hands, stretching out to an oblong shape and ensuring end is sealed to rest of dough. Carefully place each roll onto the baking sheets, spacing them evenly and leaving room for them to rise. Cover pans with plastic wrap, allow to rise one more time – about 45 minutes.

While waiting for the Persians to rise, start heating your frying oil to 350 F (180 C)

In small batches, deep fry doughnuts for a minute or two - until golden brown on the under side - before carefully flipping and frying for another 1-2 minutes on the second side.

Use a slotted metal spoon to transfer doughnuts to paper towel lined baking sheets or plates. Allow oil to come back up to temperature between batches.

Allow doughnuts to cool completely..

Whip butter , jelly, and jam together until smooth. Slowly add powdered sugar a bit at a time, until incorporated completely. Beat on high for 1 minute – mixture will be very, very thick.

Lower mixer speed to lowest setting, and slowly add milk. Once incorporated, check for consistency - you want it thick, but soft enough to spread. Add more milk or sugar to achieve the consistency you want.

Spread cooled doughnuts with frosting.

For Gluten-free: I have not yet managed to come up with a gluten-free recipe
                          that is good enough to share.

Doughnut Holes

As a Canadian living in the USA, I've had to endure powerful cravings for Canadian doughnut holes every once in a while... and discovering my gluten issues didn't do anything to stop those cravings. I came up with a quick gluten-free version back in 2012, utilizing commercially available all-purpose gluten-free flour. They were pretty ok - good, even - but were definitely not the real deal.

After much in the way of tweaking the recipe, I first came up with a great gluten-free version, and later developed a full-gluten version. Kind of backwards, I know - but now we have everyone covered! These are great in the most basic form - vanilla, unglazed doughnuts - but half the point of doughnut holes is variety. With just a few extra bowls and a small amount of effort, you can turn a basic batch of doughnut holes into a feast for the eyes AND stomach! Makes about 30 doughnut holes

Vegetable oil for frying		
Milk	1 ½ cup	375 ml
Lemon juice	2 Tbsp	30 ml
Large egg	1	1
Vegetable oil	2 tsp	10 ml
Vanilla extract	1-2 tsp	5-10 ml
All-purpose flour	2 ½ cups	625 ml
Granulated sugar	3/4 cup	175 ml
Baking soda	1 ½ tsp	7 ml
Salt	1 tsp	5 ml

Heat oil to 375 F (190 C) You can use a deep fryer, or a heavy pan. If not using a deep fryer, use a deep, heavy pot, filled to at least 3" deep.

Whisk together milk, lemon juice, egg, vegetable oil, and vanilla until well combined and smooth. In a large mixing bowl, combine remaining (dry) ingredients. Add wet ingredients to dry, stirring with a whisk until well incorporated. Allow to sit for 10 minutes.

Using two teaspoons, scoop out approximately 1" balls of dough, carefully dropping them into the hot oil. (Do NOT splash yourself!).* Cook for about 3 minutes, flip doughnut holes onto their other sides, cook for another 2-3 minutes. Cook a few donuts at a time, being careful to not over crowd your fryer / pot. When doughnut holes are cooked, use a (metal!) slotted spoon to transfer them from the oil, to a pan lined with paper towels. Once all donuts are cooked, allow to cool for a few minutes.

* Dropping the doughnut holes as described is the quickest, cleanest version - but the resulting doughnut holes will be irregular. To get nicely smooth, round doughnut holes, carefully roll the blobs of dough between moistened hands before gently adding to the hot oil.

For Gluten-Free: Mix together 1 cup sorghum flour, 2/3 cup white rice flour, 1/3 cup potato starch, 1/3 cup coconut flour, 2 tbsp tapioca starch, and 1 tsp xanthan gum. Use in place of the all-purpose flour.

Vanilla Doughnut Glaze

Water	½ cup	125 ml
Vanilla extract	½ tsp	2 ml
Salt	pinch	pinch
Icing (powdered/confectioner) sugar	3+ cups	750+ ml

Whisk together water, vanilla, and salt. Add powdered sugar, a cup or so at a time, whisking until thick (but still "dip-able") and completely smooth. Transfer to a coffee mug or other narrow/tall vessel.

Use a couple of forks to dip each (completely cooled!) donut hole – one at a time – turning to coat completely. Allow excess glaze to drip off doughnut before placing on parchment paper to dry.

Chocolate Doughnut Glaze

Water	½ cup	125 ml
Vanilla extract	½ tsp	2 ml
Salt	pinch	pinch
Cocoa powder	1/3 cup	75 ml
Icing (powdered/confectioner) sugar	2+ cups	500+ ml

Whisk together water, vanilla, and salt. Add cocoa powder, whisking until smooth. Add powdered sugar, a cup or so at a time, whisking until thick (but still "dip-able") and completely smooth. Transfer to a coffee mug or other narrow/tall vessel.

Use a couple of forks to dip each (completely cooled!) donut hole – one at a time – turning to coat completely. Allow excess glaze to drip off doughnut before placing on parchment paper to dry.

Honey Dip

Liquid honey	2/3 cup	150 ml
Water	1/4 cup	50 ml

In a medium saucepan, whisk together honey and water until honey is fully dissolved in water. Bring to a boil, turn heat down, and simmer for 3 minutes. Remove from heat, allow to cool completely before dipping cooled doughnut holes. Allow excess glaze to drip off doughnut before placing on parchment paper to dry.

Other Options/Flavours:

Sugar coated: Roll hot doughnut holes in granulated sugar. Roll cooled doughnut holes in powdered sugar.

Dutchie: Add 3/4 cup raisins to batter. Allow fried doughnuts to cool completely before dipping in vanilla doughnut glaze

Chocolate Glazed: Add 1/4 cup cocoa in place of 1/4 cup of flour (sorghum flour if gluten-free) in the batter. Allow fried doughnuts to cool completely before dipping in vanilla or chocolate doughnut glaze

Cinnamon Sugar: After rolling hot doughnut holes on paper towels - but before allowing them to cool - roll in doughnut holes in cinnamon sugar (½ cup sugar to 2 Tbsp cinnamon, or to taste)

Apple Fritter: Add 1 tsp cinnamon and a pinch of cloves to the dry ingredients. Peel and chop (about 1/4" pieces for doughnut holes, ½ " for larger fritters) 1 small apple, add to batter after wet and dry ingredients have been mixed together.

Filled/Sugared: Fit a pastry bag with a fairly wide (1/4"-½ ") metal piping tip. Fill bag with jam, pudding, or pie filling of choice. Jab metal tip into the side of a fully cooled doughnut hole, squeeze a small amount of filling into the doughnut. Roll in powdered sugar to finish.

Coconut: Dip in glaze, roll in coconut (toasted or regular)

Maple Walnut Ice Cream

Is maple walnut ice cream particularly unique to Canada? Not so far as I can tell... however, it can be hard to come by. Finding proper Maple Walnut Ice Cream can be even more difficult, and this resulted in many requests to include it in this book.

For the purist, this is made using actual maple syrup - and plenty of it! - as the sole sweetener and flavouring. It also has plenty of milk fat from the heavy cream, and additional richness from the use of a good number of egg yolks. All of this results in an ice cream that is incredibly rich and decadent. Easy to make, too!

Walnut pieces	1 1/4 cups	300 ml
Maple Syrup	1 cup	250 ml
Heavy whipping cream	2 cups	500 ml
Milk	1 cup	250 ml
Large egg yolks	6	6
Salt	½ tsp	2 ml

In a dry, nonstick saucepan, toast the walnuts over medium heat, until golden and fragrant. Allow to cool, chop. Set aside.

In a large saucepan, boil maple syrup over medium heat - stirring frequently - for 8 minutes. Add chopped walnuts, heavy cream, and milk; whisk well to combine. Bring mixture to a simmer, stir well, and remove from heat. Allow to sit for 1 hour.

In a large bowl, beat egg yolks and salt together until fluffy. Add to cooled maple mixture, whisking until smooth and combined – you don't want any unblended chunks of egg mixture.

Cook mixture over medium high; heat just to the boiling point, whisking constantly. As the mixture begins to boil, remove from heat.

Transfer mixture to a heat safe bowl. Allow to cool to room temperature before covering and transferring to the fridge. Chill overnight.

Prepare ice cream according to your ice cream maker's instructions - depending on the size of your ice cream maker, you may need to do this in batches.

Transfer ice cream to an appropriate container. Cover and freeze for at least a few hours, to firm up.

When I'm feeling extra indulgent, I'll drizzle this with maple syrup and top with toasted walnuts!

Maple Walnut Ice Cream

Tiger Tail Ice Cream

Tiger Tail Ice Cream

The lack of "Tiger Tail" - or "Tiger Tiger" depending on what area of Canada you're from - is a popular lament among Canadian expats.

This is an orange flavoured ice cream with a black licorice ribbon running throughout. Sounds weird, I know - but it's amazing. As a kid, I used to eat the ice cream from around the thickest parts of the licorice ribbon, leaving the best for last... and my homemade version did NOT disappoint, on that front.

Truth be told, I kind of shocked myself! I know I can create recipes for pretty much anything, but I thought for sure that the sweet, sort of sticky, kind of crystalline texture of the ribbon would be impossible to perfect. Nope!

Due to the way caramel is made, this recipe makes a bit more of the licorice ribbon than you'll actually need. Save some for a future batch, or heat it up slightly as an ice cream topping. It's good stuff!

Large egg yolks	6	6
Granulated sugar	1 cup	250 ml
Salt	½ tsp	2 ml
Milk	2 cup	500 ml
Heavy whipping cream	1 cup	250 ml
Orange extract	1-2 tsp	5-10 ml
Orange food colouring		
Water	1/4 cup	50 ml
Granulated sugar	½ cup	125 ml
Butter	1/4 cup	50 ml
Milk	1/4 cup	50 ml
Anise Extract	1 ½ tsp	7 ml
Black food colouring		

In a large pot, beat egg yolks together with sugar and salt until fluffy. When thoroughly combined, add a little of the milk at a time, whisking until fully incorporated and smooth – you don't want any unblended chunks of egg mixture. Add remaining milk and heavy cream, whisk until well combined.

Heat just to the boiling point, whisking constantly. Once mixture begins to boil, remove from heat. Add orange extract, stir to combine. Colour to desired tint with food colouring, set aside to cool.

Combine water and sugar in a medium sized pot. Bring to a boil, allow to simmer just until it starts to take on a golden colour.

Remove from heat, add butter carefully – it will steam and may boil up. Stir until completely melted and well combined. Add milk and anise extract, stir to combine. Tint to a deep black with food colouring, allow to cool.

Once both the ice cream mixture and the ribbon mixture are cooled to room temperature, move them to the fridge to chill overnight.

Prepare orange ice cream according to your ice cream maker's instructions. Once ice cream is finished processing, it's time to create the striping effect:

Place a few scoops of ice cream randomly in whatever container you'll be storing it in. Drizzle a scoop of licorice ribbon mixture over it, allowing it to pool in a few areas. Add a few more scoops of ice cream, pressing down lightly in a few areas to remove air pockets. Drizzle some more licorice ribbon, add more ice cream, etc. Continue to use up the rest of the ice cream – you'll likely have some licorice ribbon left over.

Cover and freeze your ice cream container for at least a few hours, to firm up before serving.

"Lunar Vapour" Ice Cream

This recipe ended up being a last minute addition to this book, as the result of a conversation with a Halifax food blogger, Lindsay of "Eat This Town". Lindsay mentioned a type of ice cream popular in Nova Scotia - one that sounded either amazing or revolting... I wasn't quite sure! Banana, Bubblegum, and Grape marbled ice cream!

After a bit of research, I was shocked that this hadn't come up when polling people for recipes to include in this book, as it appears it's wildly popular - not only in Nova Scotia, but in New Brunswick and Newfoundland too! I was shocked to hear about Newfoundland, as I'd never seen it there in the few years I lived there... but then again, I was pretty obsessed with The One True Ice Cream there: Moo Moo's Turtle Cheesecake. MMMMmm. Anyway, here we are.

This recipe is the only one I've had to do with no exposure to the source material, because logistics are absolutely in the way in this case. So, I adapted my own basic ice cream recipe to be a bit closer to commercial ice cream style (higher milk to egg yolk/heavy cream ratio than I normally go with!), and flavoured it to a nicely balanced level, using widely available flavourings. Even if this isn't exactly as the source material is, it should definitely be very close - and it'll be the closest you can come, using retail-available flavourings!

The colours I used were all Americolor gel paste colourings, in "Lemon Yellow", "Sky Blue", and "Regal Purple". The Regal Purple was mixed with a little bit of "Electric Pink" to tone down the blue in the "Regal Purple".. but this was completely optional fussiness on my part! These colours are widely available at cake decorating supply stores, as well as online... but any food colouring will work!

Makes about 8 cups / 2L ice cream

Large egg yolks	6	6
Granulated sugar	2 cup	500 ml
Salt	3/4 tsp	3 ml
Milk	3 cups	750 ml
Heavy whipping cream	3 cups	750 ml
Food colouring in yellow, blue, and purple		
LorAnn Flavour Oils in Banana Cream, Bubblegum, and Grape		

In a large pot, beat egg yolks together with sugar and salt until fluffy. When thoroughly combined, add a little of the milk at a time, whisking until fully incorporated and smooth – you don't want any unblended chunks of egg mixture. Add remaining milk and heavy cream, whisk until well combined.

Heat just to the boiling point, whisking constantly. Once mixture begins to boil, remove from heat. Divide mixture out evenly into three bowls, allow to cool to room temperature.

Once cooled, use food colouring to tint the mixture in one bowl yellow, another blue, and the third purple.

Add 1/4 tsp Banana Cream flavour oil to the yellow mixture, 1/4 tsp Bubble Gum flavour oil to the blue mixture, and 3/4 tsp Grape flavour to the purple mixture. Stir each well, rinsing the spoon off between flavours. Cover all bowls and transfer to fridge to chill overnight.

Prepare yellow ice cream according to your ice cream maker's instructions. Once it reaches a good thick ice cream texture, transfer back to the bowl and freeze. Allow ice cream maker to re-freeze for another 2 hours, or - ideally - overnight.

Prepare blue ice cream according to your ice cream maker's instructions. Once it reaches a good thick ice cream texture, transfer back to the bowl and freeze. Allow ice cream maker to re-freeze for another 2 hours or - ideally - overnight.

Prepare purple ice cream according to your ice cream maker's instructions. As it approaches the frozen stage, remove the yellow blue ice cream from the freezer.

Scoop random balls of yellow and blue ice creams into a freezer-safe dish that will hold 2L of finished ice cream. Ladle some mostly-frozen purple ice cream all over it, allowing it to flow into any crevices. Press mixture down slightly to eliminate any air holes.

Scoop more yellow and blue ice cream in, top with more purple and repeat until all of the yellow, blue, and purple ice cream is in the final container. Cover and freeze until firm.

Alternately: If that sounds like too much work - or too many dishes to wash, just layer the flavours into the final freezer container, as they come out of the ice cream maker. Just be sure to dig deep when scooping!

"Lunar Vapour" Ice Cream

Conversions

To accommodate bakers in different countries and from different cultures, measurements throughout this book have been provided in both U.S. conventional and metric. To keep things simple, measurement conversions have been rounded. See below for the exact conversions, as well as the rounded versions provided throughout this book.

Spoons	Actual Conversion*	Standard Metric Used
1/4 tsp	1.2 ml	1 ml
½ tsp	2.5 ml	2 ml
1 tsp	4.9 ml	5 ml
1 Tbsp	14.8 ml	15 ml

Cups	Actual Conversion*	Standard Metric Used
1/4 cup	59.1 ml	50 ml
1/3 cup	78.9 ml	75 ml
½ cup	118.3 ml	125 ml
2/3 cup	157.7 ml	150 ml
3/4 cup	177.4 ml	175 ml
1 cup	236.6 ml	250 ml
4 cups	946.4 ml	1000 ml / 1 liter

Ounces (Weight)	Actual Conversion*	Standard Metric Used
1 oz	28.3 grams	30 grams
2 oz	56.7 grams	55 grams
3 oz	85.0 grams	85 grams
4 oz	113.4 grams	125 grams
5 oz	141.7 grams	140 grams
6 oz	170.1 grams	170 grams
7 oz	198.4 grams	200 grams
8 oz	226.8 grams	250 grams
16 oz / 1 lb	453.6 grams	500 grams
32 oz / 2 lbs	907.2 grams	1000 grams / 1 kilogram

* Source: Google Calculator

Resources

This list is for informational purposes only, and does not necessarily constitute an endorsement of any of these companies. We do not receive payment of any kind by these companies for being listed here. It is the readers' responsibility to properly vet any companies they choose to do business with; we are not responsible for any disputes that may arise.

Ingredients

Nuts Online - www.nutsonline.com
Citric acid, gluten-free flours, nutritional yeast, nuts, tomato powder, vinegar powder, and more.

Amazon - www.amazon.com / www.amazon.ca
Citric acid, Clear Jel, cracked rye, gluten-free flours, LorAnn Oils, nutritional yeast, Prague Powder (Pink curing salt), sour cream powder, tomato powder, vinegar powder, and more

Equipment

Amazon - www.amazon.com
Cooking equipment, home brewing equipment, Zorks

Other

Celebration Generation - www.celebrationgeneration.com
Food & lifestyle blog, recipes, photos, and inspiration

Celebration Generation - Wine Making Primer
www.celebrationgeneration.com/blog/2010/12/27/wine-making-at-home-part-i-why
Learn the basics of wine making, including sanitization.

Rooftop Brew ABV Calculator
http://www.rooftopbrew.net/abv.php
Online calculator to determine final ABV% of homemade wine

Index

Marie Porter

Marie Porter is an Autistic polymath, which is just a fancy way of saying that she knows a lot of stuff - and does even more stuff - with a brain that runs on a different operating system than most. Because of that OS, her career has spanned across many facets: She's a trained mixologist, competitive cake artist, professional costumer, and - last but not least - author. As of 2017, her written works include 7 cookbooks, 6 specialty sewing manuals, and a tornado memoir. Her work has graced magazines and blogs around the world, she has costumed for Olympians and professional wrestlers, has baked for brides, celebrities, and even Klingons. Marie is now proud to share her wealth of multi-disciplinary knowledge and experience with cooks and seamstresses around the world

Michael Porter

Michael Porter works in medical manufacturing, and is a food and commercial photographer. His work has appeared in local, national, and international magazines, in catalogs, corporate websites, and as well as in many online media outlets. In addition to being an awesome husband and photographer, Michael is Celebration Generation's "Chief Engineering Officer", responsible for all custom builds, equipment repairs, and warp engine emergencies. After their home was smashed by a tornado, Michael singlehandedly built all of the cabinetry in their new kitchen! In his 'spare' time, Michael is an avid home brewer, is pursuing a degree in engineering, and is "in training" to become a Canadian.

Twisted: A Minneapolis Tornado Memoir

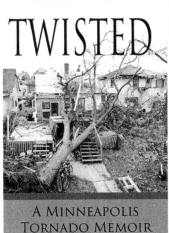

MARIE PORTER

TWISTED

A MINNEAPOLIS
TORNADO MEMOIR

On the afternoon of May 22, 2011, North Minneapolis was devastated by a tornado. Twisted recounts the Porters' first 11 months, post tornado. Rebuilding their house, working around the challenges presented by inadequate insurance coverage. Frustration at repeated bouts of incompetence and greed from their city officials. Dealing with issues such as loss of control, logistics, change, and over-stimulation, as autistic adults. With the help of social media – and the incredibly generous support of the geek community – the Porters were able to emerge from the recovery marathon without too much of a hit to their sanity levels. New friends were made, new skills learned, and a "new" house emerged from the destruction. Twisted is a roller coaster of emotion, personal observations, rants, humor, social commentary, set backs and triumphs. Oh, and details on how to cook jambalaya for almost 300 people, in the parking lot of a funeral home… should you ever find yourself in the position to do so!

The Spirited Baker
Intoxicating Desserts & Potent Potables

Combining liqueurs with more traditional baking ingredients can yield spectacular results. Try Mango Mojito Upside Down Cake, Candy Apple Flan, Jalapeno Beer Peanut Brittle, Lynchburg Lemonade Cupcakes, Pina Colada Rum Cake, Strawberry Daiquiri Chiffon Pie, and so much more.

To further add to your creative possibilities, the first chapter teaches how to infuse spirits to make both basic and cream liqueurs, as well as home made flavour extracts! This book contains over 160 easy to make recipes, with variation suggestions to help create hundreds more!

Evil Cake Overlord
Ridiculously Delicious Cakes

Marie Porter has been known for her "ridiculously delicious" moist cakes and tasty, unique flavors since the genesis of her custom cake business. Now, you can have recipes for all of the amazing flavors on her former custom cake menu, as well as many more! Once you have baked your moist work of gastronomic art, fill and frost your cake with any number of tasty possibilities. Milk chocolate cardamom pear, mango mojito.. even our famous Chai cake – the flavor that got us into "Every Day with Rachel Ray" magazine! Feeling creative? Use our easy to follow recipe to make our yummy fondant. Forget everything you've heard about fondant – ours is made from marshmallows and powdered sugar, and is essentially candy – you can even flavor it to bring a whole new level of "yum!" to every cake you make!

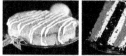

Beyond Flour
A Fresh Approach to Gluten-Free Cooking & Baking

Most gluten-free recipes are developed by taking a "normal" recipe, swapping in a simulated "all purpose" gluten -free flour... whether store bought, or a homemade version. "Beyond Flour" takes a different approach: developing the recipe from scratch. Rather than just swapping out the flour for an "all purpose" mix, Marie Porter uses various alternative flours as individual ingredients – skillfully blending flavours, textures, and other properties unique to each flour – not making use of any kind of all-purpose flour mix. Supporting ingredients and different techniques are also utilized to achieve the perfect end goal ... not just a "reasonable facsimile". With Beyond Flour, you can now indulge in some of your deepest, darkest guilty pleasure food cravings - safely and joyously!

Hedonistic Hops
The HopHead's Guide to Kitchen Badassery

While hops may seem like a bizarre or exotic item to cook with, they're really not that different from any other herb or spice in your cupboard... you just have to know what to do with them! From condiments, sides, & main dishes, to beverages and desserts, Marie Porter creates delicious recipes utilizing hops of various flavour profiles - playing up their unique characteristics - to create recipes full of complex flavour. Much like salt or lemon juice can be added to dishes to perk them up, a small amount of hops - used wisely, and with specific techniques to do so in a balanced fashion - can really make a dish sing. Even those who are not fans of beer will love the unique flavours that various types of hops can bring to their plate. Floral, earthy, peppery, citrusy...Cooking with hops is a great way to expand your seasoning arsenal!

Beyond Flour 2
A Fresh Approach to Gluten-Free Cooking & Baking

How many times have you come across a gluten-free recipe claiming to be "just as good as the normal version!", only to find that the author must have had some skewed memories on what the "normal" version tasted, looked, and/or felt like?

How many times have you felt the need to settle for food with weird after-taste, gummy consistency, or cardboard-like texture, convinced that this is your new lot in life?

Continuing where its predecessor left off, "Beyond Flour 2" is full of tasty gluten-free recipes that have been developed from scratch to be the absolute best they can be - as good or better than the "real" thing - with no "all purpose" mixes, and no need to compromise on taste or texture!

Sweet Corn Spectacular
(Minnesota Historical Society Press)

The height of summer brings with it the bounty of fresh sweet corn.Grilled or boiled, slathered in butter and sprinkled with salt, corn on the cob is a mainstay of cook-out menus. But this "vegetable" can grace your plate in so many other ways. In fact, author and baker Marie Porter once devised an entire day's worth of corn- based dishes to celebrate her "corn freak"husband's birthday. "Sweet Corn Spectacular" displays Porter's creative and flavor- filled approach to this North American original, inspiring year-round use of this versatile ingredient and tasty experimenting in your own kitchen. As Porter reminds home cooks, the possibilities are endless!

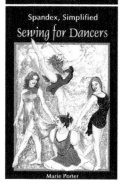